Uniquely Made

My Journey Through Christianity

Stephanie Anderson

ISBN 978-1-63903-241-9 (paperback)
ISBN 978-1-63903-242-6 (digital)

Christian Faith Publishing
832 Park Avenue
Meadville, PA 16335
www.christianfaithpublishing.com

Printed in the United States of America

Contents

Introduction

How many times have you listened to a speaker sharing part of his or her story (testimony) and felt like you could relate to the story because you have had a similar experience? And what about the times that you couldn't relate to the speaker's story? We are all uniquely made, but we still have sometimes different yet similar experiences.

You often feel less alone when someone shares an experience similar to yours. It also helps to encourage you, that if they got through such an experience, perhaps you can too. There have also been many times that what was being said sounded great and I was happy for the speaker, but the story left me feeling isolated and wondering if something was wrong with me, that no one seems to have the same experiences that I did. It made me feel as if, perhaps, I wasn't doing something right.

God let me know and wants you to know that those thoughts of inadequacy are just lies from the enemy, the devil, who wants to stop you from reaching your full potential. That is why it's so important to share your story and that is why I wrote this book. If my experiences can encourage just one person and let that person know that they are not alone and that others have gone through something similar, then this book has fulfilled its purpose.

> *And they have defeated him by the blood of the Lamb and by their testimony. And they did not love their lives so much that they were afraid to die. (Rev. 12:11)*

Salvation

Both my parents were raised Catholic, although neither was a practicing Catholic while I was growing up. My mother considered herself to be a witch and stated she didn't believe in Jesus. I pray that she has a change of heart before she dies. As for my dad, I honestly don't know for sure what he believed. It's one of the few things I truly regret. There were over a dozen times after I became a Christian that I considered talking to him about my faith, but I never had that discussion with him before he was killed in a car accident. I do know my dad had a huge, genuine, giving heart. He was just like the cliché of the person that would give somebody the shirt off his back. I like to believe that his caring heart and love for people came from a relationship with Jesus even if he didn't express that relationship with words.

If you are a Jesus follower, I implore and encourage you to pray and speak to your loved ones about where they stand with Jesus. Don't do what I did and let your cowardliness and fear of rejection stop you. Fear of rejection is from the pits of hell. The devil doesn't want anyone saved; he wants everyone to share in his misery when judgment day comes. If your family member is like my mom, don't try to nag them into faith. Pray that God will soften that person's heart and, most importantly, show them God's love. Love them where they are. You don't have to love someone's actions to love the person. We must let Jesus's light shine out of us to those around us.

YOU ARE THE LIGHT OF THE WORLD

LIKE A CITY ON A HILLTOP THAT CANNNOT BE HIDDEN

MATTHEW 5:14

No one lights a lamp and then puts it under a basket. Instead, a lamp is placed on a stand, where it gives light to everyone in the house. In the same way, let your good deeds shine out for all to see, so that everyone will praise your heavenly Father. (Matt. 5:14–16)

I was around eleven years old when I began attending church on a regular basis with a friend from my neighborhood. Most of the time, my friend's family would take me. But there were times they couldn't, so my dad would take me. I was an introvert and mostly still today. But a part of me wanted to have friends and to be part of something. That's why I attended church. I had a void in my heart that I was trying to fill. I sang in the choir, I was in youth group, I helped clean the church, I went to church camp, and I went through all the motions of what appeared to be right. I read my Bible and even had experiences of falling out at the altar and crying.

Once, my parents grounded me from going to church. I thought, *They can't take away my religious freedom.* So I got up really early in the morning, put a dress on with some sneakers, and decided to walk to church. Church wasn't just down the street; it was about an eighteen- to twenty-minute drive by car. I decided to take the back way and not walk on the main streets. It's a miracle I am alive today because I was not prepared at all for such a lengthy walk. I didn't bring anything to drink and became so desperately thirsty that I took a sip out of a Mountain Dew bottle I found on the side of the road. I had been walking for hours and still had at least a quarter of the journey to go when a car pulled up next to me and asked if I needed a ride.

The driver was a stranger, but I took the ride. I got to church with maybe twenty minutes left of it. In hindsight, I was being a dumb, unsafe, and a rebellious teenager. Thankfully, God protected me and didn't allow that to be the end of my story. My parents weren't trying to oppress my religious beliefs; they were using the only thing that would get me to pay attention. I didn't have much of a social life. Church was the only thing I really did.

I thought I was a "Christian." I didn't truly have a relationship with Christ at that point though. I don't even really remember that even being talked about much. The void in my heart was still there, and I was desperate to have it filled. I had self-worth issues also that added to the void issues. I will talk more about that in a later chapter. For now, I will say I tried to fill that void by other unhelpful means that just made things worse. My continued interactions with so-called Christians that didn't act like Christ began to harden my heart. Over several years, my heart became so hardened that I walked away from the church.

I ended up moving to a new town hours away from where I grew up. I didn't know anyone there except my fiancé and his family at the time. I transferred my job at Pizza Hut, and that was my life for a while. I got talked into going to Waffle House next store by coworkers, and it became a regular occurrence after my fiancé broke it off with me, which was for the best. I had a crush on one of the servers at Waffle House and kind of built a friendship with him and the grill guy. I started having lots of issues at my job, and they helped me get a new one. They also let me move in with them and another couple. They said they were Christians too, and we had conversations about God.

I tried going to church with them once or twice but struggled with it. See, the guy I had a crush on and the grill guy ended up being a homosexual couple. While I never felt like homosexual relationships were natural, I have had several friends throughout my life that were homosexual or bisexual. So I didn't have a problem that they were gay; my problem was in the fact the one would talk about how God told him about a woman he was supposed to marry. She was a friend in the group, and she was waiting for him. I felt so bad for her. I couldn't understand how someone could get a clear prophetic word from God about something yet ignore it for their desires, especially when it would hurt someone they claimed to love. I know he wasn't the first to do that. The Bible has many instances where people hear from God but ignore what he had to say. I guess being so close to the situation and so desperate for the void in my own life to be fulfilled, I just couldn't handle it. During the time of living with them, I did read my Bible and did journaling. I went through struggles of my own that had me confused.

I grew upset at the situation I was in. I was paying rent to sleep on a couch and have a tiny space in a closet. My roommates had no consideration for the fact that I worked on a different shift so I slept different hours. I had the one couple telling me that the new friends I made at the new job weren't good for me, especially the one guy I had grown a liking too. My final straw was when the power company came and said either I write him a check for x amount or he was turning off the power. I wrote the check, then made the decision it was time to move out. I moved back to my parents' house and lost contact with them.

I ended up with the guy that they told me I shouldn't be with. His name is Curtis, and we have been together for over nineteen years now as I write this book in 2020. You have to be very careful to who you listen to and let influence your life.

*You were running the race so well. Who has
held you back from following the truth? It certainly
isn't God, for He is the one who called you to freedom. (Gal. 5:7–8)*

Originally, Curtis and I didn't talk much about God. I believe it
was because I had mentioned my feelings on the matter at the time.

He had an aunt and uncle that were always asking us to go to
church with them. They attended several churches over the years.
About seven years into our relationship, around the end of 2008 or
beginning of 2009, I don't remember the exact time, I was jobless
and having a hard time finding work. His aunt and uncle had a
trucking business and weren't that tech-savvy, so they would ask our
help when they would have computer issues. God had also blessed
me with a gift for administration, which I didn't acknowledge at the
time. They were talking about hiring me to help with the computer/
administrative side of the business and again invited us to the current
church they were attending.

This time, for completely selfish reasons, I agreed we would
go that Sunday. I was hoping that by actually going, I would get

some favor and get the job because I was pretty desperate. Curtis was surprised but agreed. On the way, I had a panic attack. I told Curtis that I couldn't follow through with the plan. I had no clue what kind of church it was or how big, and the idea of having to interact with people freaked me out. As I said at the beginning, I have always been kind of an introvert. Curtis calmed me down as he continued to drive us to the church. After sitting in the vehicle for a bit after we got there, I finally got up the courage to go in.

The church wasn't that big and had maybe fifty or so people in it. They had video worship, which was a new concept to me since I had only dealt with live worship. They did the dreaded meet and greet where I had to interact with strangers wanting to shake my hand, hug me, and overpower my sense of smell with way too many perfumes and colognes. When it was time for the pastor to speak, I was pleasantly surprised at what he had to say. I was used to hearing messages on certain topics. The speaker would say maybe one or two verses of scripture and then basically rant on their interpretation of what the verses meant or on something else entirely. Not this pastor though. He was going through the Bible verse by verse. He would talk about different verses in more depth for a few moments. I had never heard someone share so many verses in one message. It felt like it wasn't about what he had to say but what the Word of God had to say. Despite the dislike of having to deal with others when I left, I couldn't wait to come back the next Sunday. It was so odd to me. Curtis seemed happy that I wanted to go back.

After that, we started attending church regularly. Of course, during meet and greet times, I almost always had to use the bathroom. I know that sounds silly, but it was how I managed my anxiety at the time. I never did get the job with his aunt and uncle. After so many months, they even stopped attending the church. Curtis and I stayed and got involved. The leadership had heard about our tech knowledge and asked for our help in computer-related issues.

I have heard countless salvation testimonies over the years. Some of them have extraordinary encounters with God while others, more simple. All of them were amazing in their own way. Someone accepting Christ into their life should always be celebrated! I struggled for a long time if I was really saved and had given my life to Christ despite knowing deep down that I had. There was a change in me even if it wasn't as dramatic as others. God had to remind me over and over that I was uniquely made and it was just fine that my experience wasn't like all the others I had heard.

See, with nearly every story of salvation I had heard, the person could tell the exact date they were saved. They could recount how and when it happened. This was not the case with me. I knew that over the months of attending the church, my hardened heart was slowly softened. At the end of each service, the pastor would lead the whole congregation in a salvation prayer said out loud. I cannot tell you which one of those many times I said it that it fully happened, but I know without a doubt that it did sometime in the first half of 2009.

For me it wasn't just about one particular moment in time, it was about a gradual but transformative lifestyle change. See, our journey doesn't end the moment we get saved; it is the beginning of an even better journey.

If you haven't started on this journey yet, I pray today that your eyes and heart would open for you to see that you need a savior and that you ask Jesus to be that savior. Just call on his name. You don't have to clean up your act or try to be a better person or do anything except believe and call on his name! It's really that simple. Here is a sample prayer you could say or get inspiration from:

> *Jesus, I know I have failed you and I ask for your forgiveness. I believe that you came and died on the cross for my sins. Jesus, I surrender to you. Be my Savior and transform me to live for you. Amen.*

> *For everyone who calls on the name of the* Lord *will be saved. (Rom. 10:13)*

If you have made the decision for Jesus Christ to be your savior today, I would love to celebrate with you and send you some resources for your next steps on this new journey. Send me an email at writersa.info@gmail.com.

Self-Worth and Relationships

I am going to be brutally honest in this chapter, and parts of it might be hard for some to handle, but sometimes life is hard to handle. It's a miracle that I am alive today and in such a good place because things could have gone completely different if I didn't have God's mercy, grace, and love in my life. I have no doubt that people had been praying for me and that God had greater plans than some of the circumstances I was dealt. He has turned all of it for his and my good.

Ever heard the saying, "Sticks and stones may break my bones but words will never hurt me"? I heard it growing up, and I can say it's another one of those lies from the devil. Words are powerful. Read Genesis. There was nothing, and God spoke and created everything. There are many scriptures talking about the power of the tongue and the words you speak. Here are just a few:

> *The tongue can bring death or life; those who love to talk will reap the consequences. (Prov. 18:21)*

> *Gentle words are a tree of life; a deceitful tongue crushes the spirit. (Prov. 15:4)*

> *It's not what goes into your mouth that defiles you; you are defiled by the words that come out of your mouth. (Matt. 15:11)*

Wondering why I brought this up? I have endured verbal abuse since I can remember. I have been picked on and bullied by countless number of people. Some act as if they were joking, but it all would cut or reopen wounds that had never fully healed. As a young child, one is very impressionable and doesn't understand that when someone puts you down it's normally from their own insecurities and has very little to actually do with you. By the time one gets old enough to know, the damage has already been done.

As a child, I was told by adults and peers that I was useless, worthless, fat, ugly, stupid, and other worse things I will not repeat. Hearing it from your peers hurts but not as much as having someone that is supposed to be older, wiser, and caring. I will not name names because it would do no good. I will say I have forgiven them and prayed for them. I took the false truths to heart, and as a result I had no self-worth, no self-esteem, or self-confidence. When you have none of those, it tends to lead you to do things that are not good for you. You are more susceptible to peer pressure and follow bad influences. I also never felt like I fit in anywhere, and so to try to connect with others, I would do things or let others do things that I knew in my heart I shouldn't. Like I mentioned in a previous chapter, I had a void I was trying to fill with what the world says a person needs.

When I hit puberty, around ten things got worse. I was already having issues with what people thought of me and such but now add hormones and a changing body that I was already very self-conscious about. By then I had already seen porn magazines and learned about sex and had a skewed idea of what a woman should look like to attract a man. My chest developed faster than most of the girls my age, which of course got the attention of the hormonal boys too. As I said before I didn't really fit into any group. I wasn't popular, or nerdy, or Goth, or anything. I basically felt like an outsider, a nobody. Sure, some people would talk to me, and I was part of Girl Scouts for a while, but I really never connected with people. I always hide my true feelings and thoughts. Now that my chest developed though, boys that wouldn't give me the time of day before gave me some attention, and I would feed off it even if it was the wrong attention. They would play these games of who could cop a feel, which was sexual harassment and truly not okay. I was so attention starved and wanted someone to like me that I just let them do it. I never said no, never stopped them, and never told anyone. I know, of course, I should have done all of those things.

I became part of a youth group at church that I was going to with a girlfriend. One would think that would be a good thing, right? Yeah, in reality it led me down a destructive path that would last way too long. I am not against youth groups, hear me out. They can be very helpful to most, and honestly, it wasn't all bad. There were seeds planted in the times of ministry that would grow later. However, for me, I was introduced to a group of guys that weren't good for me. I got my first "boyfriend." It wasn't really a relationship and didn't last long. It was more like he liked my body and my willingness to let him do things like get to "third base." If anyone felt like they might get struck down by God, it was me because I didn't go on actual dates with this guy. Everything we did happened inside the church. I enjoyed the attention, but it did nothing for the void I had. If anything, I believe it helped to harden my heart.

My next boyfriend when I was twelve was nineteen years old and also from the youth group. Again, we only hung out at church and youth group events until one day when my parents went out of town to a Rolling Stones concert. Yes, my parents left me alone when I was twelve years old. Do not judge them as bad parents for that. Times were different back then, plus I acted to all those around me as a well-grounded, responsible person. In reality, it was all an act. I was a really good liar. Not only did I hide my feelings from the people around me, but I lied to myself about a lot of things too. Back to being alone by myself, the boyfriend came over and I lost my virginity. He did not know it because, like I said, I was a good liar and didn't want to give him the privilege of knowing the truth. He didn't deserve it. I wasn't in love with him, and he really wasn't that good of a person to me, but I thought if I had sex, something would change. You read about how great it is and so on; but in reality, when it's not with the right person, it's meaningless. Afterward, I felt even more empty and depressed than I was before.

After he left, I went to a very dark place. I felt like the void was never going to fill. No one was actually going to ever love me or want to truly be with me. The world would be a better place if I didn't exist. I wouldn't be a burden on those around me if I was dead. I had enough with this world and wrote a goodbye note to my family. I thought of three different ways to try to end my life. First were pills. God gave me an extreme gag reflex though, and so when I tried to take a bunch of them, I ended up just throwing them up. Next was to put a bag over my head, but the bag ended up breaking. Finally, I took a pointed steak knife and was going to pierce my heart. But instead of doing it quickly, I slowly pushed it against my chest. When it pierced the skin, two things stopped me. First, it hurt, and second, I knew it was going to make a mess and didn't want others to have to deal with that. I know now God saved me that night because he wasn't done with me yet.

I would love to say I had a beautiful revelation then and I never thought of suicide again, but that is simply not the truth. I had cleaned up after my attempts to take my life so my parents wouldn't find out. I had to try to keep up the happy, responsible, good-girl act. I made one minor mistake though in my cleaning: I forgot to throw out the goodbye note. My parents ended up finding it and made me go to a psychologist. At the psychologist, they made me answer a questionnaire. I lied on it and answered the questions how I thought they would want me too. See, I felt pretty positive that if anyone knew what I truly thought and felt, they would throw me into a padded room, lock the door, and throw away the key. I talked with the person, and it didn't help the way I was feeling at all. I was diagnosed with antisocial disorder, manic depressive (also known as bipolar), and a male-dependency complex. I was given different drugs to take that were supposed to help me out. Help they did not. I can't really describe the feeling I had when I was on them, but I can say I felt even worse than before. They tried different ones and doses, but I couldn't stand how I felt and who I was on them, so I started just flushing the daily dose down the toilet and pretending I took them. I realized how people wanted me to act and what they wanted to hear; thus, I did that to get them off my back.

I knew in my heart there was nothing anyone on this earth could do to fix me. Even though I went to church, read my Bible, and had encounters with God, it just never clicked back then that he loved me and would heal my brokenness. If you are reading this right now and are struggling with brokenness in your heart that you feel can't be fixed, please listen to the truth of God. He loves you unconditionally. He doesn't want you to be broken. He wants to heal you. You don't have to wait for over twenty years like I did. Learn to let God have it all. In your heart, forgive those that have hurt you and, most importantly, forgive yourself. When you forgive someone, it's not for their benefit. It's for your benefit. You don't even have to tell the person you forgive them. Please don't confuse giving it to God and forgiving someone as forgetting it ever happened. You don't need to forget because forgetting allows a chance for them to do it again. Forgiving is not allowing what they did to affect your life any further. Forgiving takes the power away they and the devil have over you. Forgiveness isn't a feeling; it's a choice you have to make and repeat that choice.

> *Then Peter came to him and asked, "Lord, how often should I forgive someone who sins against me? Seven times?" "No, not seven times," Jesus replied, "but seventy times seven!" (Matt. 18:21–22)*

> *Give all your worries and cares to God, for he cares about you. (1 Pet. 5:7)*

He
HEALS
the
brokenhearted and
bandages
their
wounds.

PSALM 147:3

So humble yourselves before God. Resist the
devil, and he will flee from you. Come close to God,
and God will come close to you. (James 4:7–8)

It ended with the nineteen-year-old eventually too. There was
another boy at church that was only two years older than me that I
felt sorry for because he had lost his mother to cancer. Despite the
fact that he treated me badly in front of others, he had another side
in private and I could see his brokenness. He would open up to me
and talk about what was on his heart and how he was feeling. We
would talk all night on the phone, even fall asleep on the line, and
wake up to each other. There were no cell phones then. We had to
use corded landlines, which means if anyone else tried to call, they
couldn't. And there was no speakerphone either. You had to hold that
thing to your ear the entire time. I was around fourteen at this time,
and he had a car. We only got to see each other at church. He was
the drummer for the worship band. On multiple occasions, when he
was done with worship, we would sneak out. He would drive us to

some secluded road, and we would have sex. We would make sure to be back before service was over. We were not even technically a couple because he said he didn't want a girlfriend and I just went along with it. I was still trying to fill my void, and I thought maybe if I couldn't fix myself, I could help fix him. It doesn't work that way though. You can't fix someone's brokenness, especially with worldly things. Eventually, we ended things in an unpleasant way because he took interest in another girl at church. I don't remember the specifics really, but I remember how I felt and how he made a nasty scene about not wanting anything to do with me. As I said at the beginning, he wasn't ever that nice to me around others, and when he got confronted about possibly being with me, he denied it because he didn't want to ruin his reputation or something. Not only was I rejected, but I was humiliated and felt like a lesser person. When told over and over with words and by people's actions that you are ugly and worthless, it's hard not to believe that as the truth if you aren't grounded in the truth of God.

Each circumstance hardened my heart more to people. I let people use me time and time again until I eventually had a breaking point. See, I was also a generous person that would help anyone that asked. I would give away my lunch money and go without if I thought it would help. I am not bragging here; I am trying to paint a picture of who I was at that time. That despite all the hurtfulness and rejection I went through, I tried to help others still. Part of it was trying to be a good person, but honestly, part of it was to feel useful and be part of something.

I believe my breaking point, when I gave up on the idea that I would ever fit in anywhere or anyone would actually care about me, was on my fifteenth birthday. A group of my so-called friends had agreed to go watch a movie together to celebrate. My dad drove me to the movie theater. I lied about seeing one of my friends so he would leave. I was a teenager and that's what we did. I got my ticket to see *The First Wives Club*, then waited and waited and waited for my "friends" to show. The movie was starting, and I went in the theater alone. I sat through that movie crying nearly the entire time. After the movie, while I was waiting for my dad to pick me up, I saw the "friends" coming out of another theater, happy, laughing, and having a great time without me. They didn't know I saw them, and since I wasn't a confrontational person, I didn't make a scene. When I saw them at school, they all made some excuse of why they couldn't make it. I knew the truth though. After that, sweet Stephanie was heartless and hated everyone. Or at least, that's how I felt.

I did end up with a new nickname, Queen B. Not referring to honey either, if you get my drift. I pretended even more than I already had that I didn't care what others thought of me. The truth was I felt dead inside and numb to life. At times, when alone, not knowing how to release what was inside of me and to feel something, I would hurt myself. I would dig my fingernails into my hand or thighs. I would punch my thighs as hard as I could. I had constant thoughts of suicide. *I wish I had never been born. Why was I here when no one wanted me?*

I was still going to church and going through the motions of what I thought others wanted out of me so I wouldn't be put back on drugs or be locked up. I don't recall how it happened, but the girlfriend I mentioned that got me going to church had a cousin who was ten years older than us, and I ended up starting a relationship with. I didn't find him attractive or truly have feelings for him, but I didn't want to be alone, and he was willing to be with me. He worked at an orange grove and only had a third-grade education. He couldn't barely read or write. I felt like he was the best I could do. At least, he didn't mind being seen in public with me. We went to church several times but did not receive a loving welcome. No one was keen on a fifteen-year-old dating a twenty-five-year-old. We eventually just stopped going to church, and our relationship also caused a rift in the relationship I had with the girl that I went to church with. My parents weren't so happy about it either but for some reason allowed it. They did make me get on birth control via a shot because they knew I wasn't trustworthy with taking pills. My boyfriend eventually got laid off from his job and moved in with us. He had a hard time finding a job that would hire him. I ended up getting a job at Pizza Hut, my first job, to try to help and pay his bills.

School was nearly intolerable to me at this point. I had no friends, and being in the classes I was made things even harder. I was in an easy science that was boring to me, and I kept falling asleep. I would do so well on tests that everyone else in the class hated me because I ruined the curve. Then I was in an advanced math class where I was only one of two juniors. The rest were seniors. They didn't seem to have an issue with the other junior but hated me for some reason and were quite mean to me. Two months before the end of my junior year, I decided to drop out and just work full time.

My coworkers weren't the best influences for me either. Most were older and were into the party scene. To try to fit in, I agreed to do things I shouldn't have. For example, after work one night, someone brought in a cinnamon alcohol. As we were cleaning up for the night, we drank. I was only sixteen at the time, and the only alcohol I had prior was a sip or two of my dad's beer, which was nasty, I might add. Another time, one asked me to go to a club. Being in crowds gave me immense anxiety, plus I was not a dancer, but she said she didn't want to go alone. She was old enough to drink, and the second we got to the club, she started drinking. Maybe thirty or so minutes after being there, she said she was going to the bathroom and told me to wait where I was. I awkwardly waited for over an hour on the side of the dance floor trying to not make eye contact with anyone and not completely freak out. I had no clue where the bathroom was or what had happened. For all I knew, she abandoned me. All the worst-case scenarios played through my head. After what seemed like eternity, a stranger came up to me and told me my friend was sick in the bathroom. It was obvious she got alcohol poisoning from overdrinking. I had my license, so I could legally drive. However, her vehicle was a stick shift. It took me at least fifteen minutes to just back out of the parking lot because I kept stalling it out. Once we started going, I had no clue on directions because we were in West Palm Beach, a larger town I had never been to before. I took us through a not-so-good part of the town before finally getting to the interstate to make it back up to where we lived. I had never driven on an interstate before. My already elevated anxiety skyrocketed to new heights. I never went to a club again. I did go to the local billiard hall with my coworkers a few times. My boyfriend wasn't so happy about it. He didn't like me interacting with other people really. I did end up having sex with one of my coworkers. It meant nothing, and I felt nothing. It was all meaningless, just like how life felt to me at the time. The truth was that, while to others my boyfriend seemed like he loved me and cared for me, he was both verbally and physically abusive. I won't lie, I would dish back some hurtful words too, but I didn't deserve how I was treated. If I told him I didn't want to have sex, he didn't care and would hold me down and rape me. Why did I stay with him? As I said before, I didn't think I could do better or even deserve better.

When you don't know your self-worth in Christ, you fall into the lies of the enemy. Even though I had read the Bible numerous times by this point in my life, I had no true revelation of the meaning of the words. It was planted in my heart but was still hidden at the time. I was so stuck on myself, and woe is me that I couldn't hear God's small, still voice because I had yet to genuinely surrender to God. The only time I felt his peace was when I went to the beach. It was my safe haven, you could say. It was the one place that I could forget about everything else. The horrible world didn't exist there for me. It was a place of beauty and wonder. I felt alive there.

After nearly four years together, we got engaged. My fiancé had a family in north Florida, which was rural and a completely different culture than the beach area. The only aspect that I enjoyed about it was that there were less people. My parents had enjoyed taking drives up to that area for the longest time, even prior to my relationship with this man; hence, it wasn't a big surprise when they decided to buy ten acres of land up there and place a manufactured home on it. My dad was a postal worker though, and trying to get a transfer was not easy. Because they couldn't move until he did, the momentous decision was made that my fiancé and I would move up there and take care of the place. My boss at Pizza Hut aided me in getting a transfer to one up in that area. He was disappointed that I was leaving though as he had plans on making me a shift manger. I found that odd since I didn't see myself as being a leader at all. I was good at math, which came in handy for the paperwork side of managing the work that I had been helping with.

We moved, and I worked as much as I could since I had to pay all the bills because he still had not gotten any job. He spent more and more time with his family. He didn't want me to do anything other than work or go shopping. I was invited to a New Year's Eve party but couldn't go because of him. I was getting fed up with him controlling me, and we got into fights all the time. Until one day I came home late from a long night of work to a voice mail on the house phone. The voice mail stated that I did not need to go over to his family's house the next morning because he needed a break from me and was going to come get some of his things. Later I would find out he was having an affair with his sister-in-law. I was a little sad but mostly angry after all I gave up and did for him. It didn't take me long to figure out that this was truly a blessing, and I was done with him. There was no going back to how things were. I could not live like that anymore. For months, my life consisted of going to work, the store when needed, and home. It was so bad that when coworkers asked me to go to Waffle House with them after work one night, about six months after I moved, I had to ask where it was. They looked at me in shock. It was two buildings over from the Pizza Hut. We could walk there. Little by little I started to hang out with my coworkers and at Waffle House.

My ex-fiancé started harassing me, showing up at my work after calling my house literally hundreds of times. He apologized and wanted me to take him back, but I made it very clear it was not going to happen. One night he showed up at my parents' house while I had a male friend over that I was interested in. He said he wanted his shotgun back, so I gave it to him and told him to leave. A few minutes later he barged back into the house, freaking out and threatening to kill himself. My heart was so hardened at that point that the first thing that crossed my mind was what a mess that would make and it would ruin my parents' house. I got him to leave the house, and he said that I should not be surprised if I hear he is found dead on the side of the road. I thought, *Well, at least I wouldn't have to deal with it.* I know that sounds extremely heartless, and it was, but I was in a very dark place with all the abuse I had endured from him. I had not reached a healing, forgiving place yet. I was in such a dark, wrathful place that I even wrote a story about killing him and getting away with it and then killing several others that had wronged me over the years. Thank God I only killed them on paper and never went insane enough to attempt any of it. He didn't kill himself, by the way, but he did continue to harass me. I could never prove it, but my truck stopped working, and upon thorough examination, it was discovered it was tampered with. I believe it was him hoping I would call him for help. I'd rather walk home than do that. I almost did once, but one of the workers at the Waffle House I became friends with got his brother to take me home. I was quite grateful about that since it was a twenty-minute drive using the interstate, so walking the back ways would have probably taken me hours and would have been quite dangerous especially after midnight.

As for relationships during this time, I did end up hooking up with the guy that was at my house when my ex showed up for a little bit. But he ended up with a different coworker, which caused some drama. I had a one-night stand with a Pizza Hut employee from another store that was temporarily working at ours because we were shorthanded. I told him there were no strings attached and such, but I guess he didn't believe me or didn't want to be around me because he didn't show up for any of his shifts after.

I did become a shift manager for the Pizza Hut. It was a little awkward to me because I didn't feel like I should be leading anyone. The store manager wanted to be everyone's friend, and even when I tried to discipline someone for doing their job seriously wrong, it was overturned by him. It became immensely stressful to work there. I would hang out with the few coworkers I got along with. We drank too much and smoked pot mostly. I did cocaine once, but thank God I couldn't stand how I felt when I was on it, so I could easily say no the next time. I also tried a "double roll" once. Later I found out it was ecstasy.

As I mentioned in the first chapter, I sought help in getting a new job so I could get away from all that, at least that was the hope. I even moved in with my friends from Waffle House so I didn't have to drive so far back and forth to work. When I was first hired at a call center for Dell desktops technical support, I knew very little about computers and it was a temporary position. There was a day shift and an evening shift that overlapped for a couple hours. There was a lady that was older than me on the day shift that I did not get along with. We got into little arguments all the time. After a few months, the temporary job was done and several of us got hired full time. I was grateful but surprised that I got hired on full time. The temporary job had only one focus, which was a bios update, so my knowledge on computers in general was still quite limited. They were in desperate need of techs though, so we didn't get the normal two-week training. Instead, we got a crash course on just the program to input the call information for three days. At the end of the three days, we were to be placed on teams. But instead of placing people with their teams, they placed them wherever there was a free computer. The lady that I had issues with and I looked at each other as they placed the first few people and made the decision we didn't want to be stuck alone, so we insisted they place us next to each other. We set aside our issues for a common goal, and after that, we became good acquaintances. We learned how to bribe the L2 techs (the ones that walked around answering questions the other techs couldn't figure out) to help us more willingly. We had a bowl of candy. We even got some help from first shift before they left because of the candy.

When I first started working at the company, I ended up hanging out with some guys there. Later on, I would learn that one had an interest in me only because I looked like his ex-girlfriend. I nearly always had a tendency to hang out with boys growing up. I mean I had a few girlfriends; but I was more comfortable around boys, perhaps because I felt there was less judgment, there was less drama, and I was a tomboy. As I said before, I was daddy's girl so I learned how to work on vehicles, rebuild engines, and a lot of hands-on things like that. I was even in auto mechanics in high school, and the boys hated me because I knew more about vehicles than they did.

Back to hanging out with guys from work. They all were around my age, and we would either go somewhere to eat and talk or go hang out at someone's house. One of them had gotten out a jail, claimed to be lonely, and showed interest in me. Of course, I was the only female so not too surprising. I ended up following him back to his house, and we had sex. We hooked up a few more times but tried not to let anyone know. Again, I wasn't good enough to be seen, only to have sex with. Someone eventually noticed us both driving off in same direction, I guess, and said something to the guy. He had a complete fit. He accused me of telling people, which was totally not true. I didn't want to admit that to anyone. Things got really odd with him after that. It got to the point that if I walked into a room, he would leave. I told one person about it, and they didn't believe me, so we set up an experiment. The person went into the break room and started having a conversation with the guy. A few minutes later, I walked into the room, not going anywhere near them, mind you, and the dude just left mid-conversation. The other person was shocked. It didn't hurt my feelings. Actually, I found it kind of funny.

I still hung out with the group of guys. One night someone went to get rolls (ecstasy) and came back with gel tabs. I did not know what they were but didn't want to be a party pooper, so I took one. It had me all messed up and for good reason. I would later find out that it was a large dose of LSD. I can say it was the last illegal drug I ever had. I thank God to this day that I never became addicted to any of the drugs or alcohol especially when addiction runs in the family. One could say, though, my addiction was sex. I was in the hope that perhaps one time it would live up to all the hype people gave it. Later on, I would learn it is only truly satisfying when it is in the context of how God created it: for it to be an intimate moment with a person that loves you completely with no ulterior motive and that you love back the person the same way.

This explains why a man leaves his father and mother and is joined to his wife, and the two are united into one. (Gen. 2:24)

I did end up having a one-night stand with one other guy, and again, things got awkward. After that, I made a declaration to myself that I would rather be single and celibate the rest of my life than deal with anymore drama. I didn't realize it at the time; but when I did that, even though I didn't have a relationship with God at the time, I was releasing that aspect of my life to him. I knew that the choices I made in that area were all bad, so it was best for me not to make them anymore. God had it all worked out, and I was fortunate enough not to have to wait long for him to reveal the beginning of his plans. Around this time I did start reading some of my Bible again.

At work, there was this guy that during lunch and after work sat on the picnic bench outside and would talk to anyone that would listen. He was a full-on geek and would nerd talk just about anything. Half the time I had no clue what he was talking about, but I was enthralled. I couldn't get enough. I noticed that he would say the same thing in different ways, gauging the audience reaction to make sure everyone got it. One day this guy asked me to a LAN party. I had no clue what that was, but I agreed without hesitation. He asked several people, not just me. One of them was Dave, a guy I hung out regularly with and who acted like a brother I never had. The party was at the house of a first shifter I knew. I would later find out he had a crush on me and freaked out a little when I showed up. When I got there, I found out LAN stood for Local Area Network. Meaning, people brought their computers together and played games. This was in the days of dial-up, so it was much easier to take your full desktop somewhere than try to get anything to play over the Internet. The downside though at times was, with moving the systems sometimes, things would stop working right; so instead of getting to play, you spent the whole time trying to fix it. This was the case for this party, and by the time it was figured out, everyone had to leave. It was cool hanging out and learning more with them, plus I kind of had a crush on the guy that invited me, so anytime I got with him was awesome.

Not long after that, at work, they finally arranged the teams to all be together. When they did that, I found out I was on the same team as Dave and the guy I had a crush on named Curtis. The three of us started hanging out more and more. Around the same time, I moved back to my parents' house. My mom was living there, but my dad still hadn't got a transfer. He was only able to come up once in a while on his days off.

One day I admitted to Dave that I really liked Curtis but was too chicken to ask him out. Dave agreed to do it for me the next day at work. The next day Dave didn't show up for work. I was so frustrated and mentioned it to someone else, and they agreed to ask for me instead. In hindsight, the whole situation was embarrassing, but it makes for a funny story. As he went to ask him, a female coworker asked which guy it was. I pointed to Curtis, and she said he is kind of cute. It was like my eyes were fully opened for the first time because up till that point I never even paid attention to his looks. It was his personality and heart I fell for. This was a big deal to me since I know this will sound bad, but I totally judged guys on if I thought they were doable before this. It was completely different with this guy. Until she said that, it hadn't even crossed my mind. The only thing on my mind was I wanted more time with him. The guy that asked for me came back and told me Curtis said we would need to talk after work. I was so nervous and anxious the rest of the night. When clock-out time came, I was still on a call, and without saying anything to me, Curtis left. I freaked out. First off, it was rare that he wasn't the last on the phone, but also, he said we needed to talk. I was crushed and assumed him not saying anything was his answer.

The next day I was on edge to see him and how he would react to me. I was a little shocked that he acted like nothing was different. He had to do something for his dad after work the night before and just forgot about it. It was the first lesson of many that I would realize that he isn't a great multitasker and forgets everything else when his mind is focused on one particular task. He was so different than any other guy I knew. We had our talk, and he basically said that he was good with having a relationship and that either things would work out or I would probably end up hating him. He didn't know me fully but could tell I had a lot of baggage and brokenness, and if he could help, he would. As I mentioned in a previous chapter, he had a relationship with God I didn't know about at the time so he had way more insight into things. I would later find out, also that on that day he said yes to going out with me, that he made the commitment in his heart that him saying yes to going out to me was equivalent to him saying yes to marrying me. He would stay with me forever or until I tell him to

29

leave. His relationship journey was so different than mine. He was twenty-one years old and only had three girlfriends. Of the three girlfriends, only one was a real relationship where they dated outside of school, and it lasted more than a few days. He was so disciplined that he had only ever kissed a couple of girls. I had never met a guy especially at that age that would openly admit to being a virgin and proud of it. Honestly, I wasn't sure why he would lie, but I had a hard time believing it. The first time we made out, I went into it thinking, *I am taking things slow this time. I will not let it go too far no matter what.* God is so amazing in how he works things. After kissing for a bit, we started talking and both admitted that we had been thinking the same thing, that it wasn't going to go further than kissing. I remember laughing so much about how it went down and being so happy that this guy seemed to want me for me the person and not my body alone.

Dave, Curtis, and I became a trio of friends that would hang out after work and on days off. On February 16, 2001, the three of us were hanging out at Dave's place. It had gotten really late, so we decided to just stay the night there. Curtis and I were to sleep in the living room. Dave woke us up the next day, asking how in the world we could sleep facing each other on the couch. We had to work that day, and my vehicle was still at work, so Curtis gave me a ride to my house so that I could change clothes. We were pulling into my parents' driveway when I saw my dad's vehicle and was like, "Hey, my dad came up." Curtis had a weird expression on his face that I would later find out was him freaking out a bit about what might happen. See, my parents had ten acres and a long driveway before you reached the house, and it was kind of redneck like. Curtis, having been brought up in the South, had all type of images of how things could go wrong. Not to mention, most that met my dad got a little intimated because he was six feet four inches and weighed like three hundred plus pounds. He kind of looked like a Viking. What most didn't know was that he was basically a big teddy bear. It was my short mom with her cane that was the scary one. I introduced them and left him in the living room with my parents while I changed. They seemed to get along just fine. We left for work; and that night, after work, things changed between us. He ended up coming home with me and staying the night. We didn't have sex. We just didn't want to be apart from each other. After that night, we were together nearly 24-7 for four months until our work wouldn't let us both have days off to go to a family reunion that his family was holding in a different state.

Both being uniquely made, we had our differences. We grew up different too, and our perspectives on certain issues weren't the same. Yes, sometimes we would get into disagreements that even led to shouting and such, but we never stewed in those things though.

And don't sin by letting anger control you. Don't
let the sun go down while you are still angry, for
anger gives a foothold to the devil. (Eph. 4:26–27)

Our relationship worked well because we were real with each other from the start. Too many times I have heard or knew people that will act one way while dating and then when they get married, change to reveal who they really are. We originally said we wouldn't get married. Marriage to us at the time was just a formality. We were the odd couple that most who knew us didn't understand why we were together. We didn't even look like we should be together. He was tall and skinny; I was short and overweight. His friends that were superficial questioned him on why he was with me. Knowing that they wouldn't understand the real reasons, he gave them the superficial response of, "Did you see her chest?" It would be years later that one of his friends, in the middle of the night, when I was with them helping build counters for his business, would say, "I get it now." We didn't conform to what society said we should be and do because it wasn't who we were.

We did eventually get married Christmas Day 2003. It was spontaneous. We just felt like it was something we should do one day, and a couple weeks later, we did. It was a very small informal event at my aunt's house, and my notary mom performed it. We let her even pick out what would be said and all. The next day his parents threw a reception at their house because his family didn't get the chance to be involved with the wedding. We didn't care to make a big deal out of it because for us it didn't change who we are since in our hearts we had already made the commitment. It did whoever change how people perceived us as we showed the world that commitment.

> *And he said, "This explains why a man leaves his father and mother and is joined to his wife, and the two are united into one. Since they are no longer two but one, let no one split apart what God has joined together." (Matt. 19:5–6)*

Ten years after we got married and we had been through so much (a bit of it is told in other chapters), we decided to have a formal vow renewal. The Matthew scripture was dear to my heart since so many circumstances tried to split us apart. When we first got married, I didn't have a relationship with God. I didn't understand the importance of being unified by God. The renewal was a celebration of what God had gotten us through over all those ten years of marriage. Not all couples that had gone through similar circumstances made it through together.

As I write this, we are a couple months away from our seventh wedding anniversary and four months from being a couple for twenty years. Every day I am grateful for God putting us together and strengthening us as a couple. I thought we had a good relationship to start with; but once I gave my heart to God and we put God first in our lives, including our relationship as a couple, things got even better. We have been able to grow together and see God's hand on our lives in all aspects. We still don't agree on everything—and never will. However, we communicate better and are able to use the Holy Spirit to try to understand each other's perspective. Some of the most important lessons people need to learn about relationships of any type is that they should always be evolving/growing and that it each has to put equal effort while taking responsibility for the actions they do. The blame game has and will continue to destroy relationships.

> *Do to others as you would like them to do to you. (Luke 6:31)*

Get rid of all bitterness, rage, anger, harsh words, and slander, as well as all types of evil behavior. Instead, be kind to each other, tenderhearted, forgiving one another, just as God through Christ has forgiven you. (Eph. 4:31–32)

People who conceal their sins will not prosper, but if they confess and turn from them, they will receive mercy. (Prov. 28:13)

I was with a man that I loved, loved me for me, treated me right, wasn't abusive in anyway, encouraged me, helped me through my issues; also, I had a relationship with God and knew that he loved me and forgave me. I should have been happy, right? The depression and feeling like a constant failure doesn't exist anymore, right? The thoughts of suicide should have been gone, right? Wrong. It was a daily struggle despite everything. The littlest thing would set me off. I would cry my eyes out, self-harm at times, and want to die. It didn't matter how great my life was, I still felt unworthy, lesser than others, had no self-confidence or self-esteem. I hid it from nearly everyone. Most people thought I was happy-go-lucky. I bottled things up and would wallow in my misery. I was negative about everything for so long I didn't know how to change.

One day I heard a message on the radio that said if you focus on everything that is negative, guess what? That's all you see and actually help make more negative happen. If you focus on keeping a positive attitude about what you are doing, now all of a sudden, the things you thought would never happen happens.

Humanly speaking, it is impossible. But with God everything is possible. (Matt. 19:26)

When I heard that, it really hit home for me, and from that moment on, I decided to focus on the positive. Am I perfect at it? No. Is my life perfect? That's a big *no*. Is it harder when the circumstances are rougher? Yes. But instead of lingering on the negative, I try to think of something positive instead. These are just a few scriptures that I would meditate on to help change my thinking:

>*Always be joyful. Never stop praying. Be thankful in all circumstances, for this is God's will for you who belong to Christ Jesus. (1 Thess. 5:16–18)*

>*Don't copy the behavior and customs of this world, but let God transform you into a new person by changing the way you think. Then you will learn to know God's will for you, which is good and pleasing and perfect. (Rom. 12:2)*

>*Let all that I am praise the Lord; may I never forget the good things he does for me. He forgives all my sins and heals all my diseases. He redeems me from death and crowns me with love and tender mercies. (Ps. 103:2–4)*

>*Let no corrupting talk come out of your mouths, but only such as is good for building up, as fits the occasion, that it may give grace to those who hear. (Eph. 4:29)*

It did improve my health and life; however, the root of the issue was still there. Those moments of debilitating depression and wishing I was dead still happened. I tried everything I could. I prayed for deliverance, read my Bible multiple times, read other books, listened to messages, and so on. I felt like I was going to be stuck with it forever. I didn't understand why I couldn't get free from it. I would also feel condemned about it because I was a Christian and a leader in the church. Was I a fraud? What would others say if they found out? I hid. I didn't even tell Curtis the full truth. I walked with my head down and tried to avoid eye contact with others. Even though I was surrounded by people that loved me, I felt so alone most of the time. I would put on a false smile and pretend all was okay.

In January 2018, about nine years since I gave my life to God, our church was doing its annual first of the year twenty-one days of fasting. At the end of it, our church had gotten several of the leaders tickets to go to an awakening revival being held at a large church that was over a two-hour drive away. Curtis and I were planning on going together, but his job needed him to work late. I had no ride, and at that point, I also no longer had anyone to watch my kids. I tried calling several people that intended on going and others that might be able to watch the kids if I did find a ride. Nothing was working out. I was getting no answers or it wasn't an option. I felt so desperate. I was in tears because I felt in my spirit that it was very important for me to attend. After exhausting all my options, I had nearly given up hope. God worked it out though. At the last moment, my pastor figured out that even though it would be a tight fit, I could ride with the group in his truck. His wife made it back in town just in time to get my kids and take them to their place with their kids until Curtis got off work.

We got there and were seated in the top row middle of stadium-seating-style church that can hold a couple thousand, I would guess. I got a seat in the middle of our group. I remember during worship my back was hurting so much that I almost sat down, but when they sung their version of "Surrounded (Fight My Battles)" by Upperroom, I just pressed through. I got a warm sensation down my back, and the pain subsided. Steven Furtick was the guest speaker that night, and he gave a good message. At the end of the service though, Stovall Weems got up said that he felt the Holy Spirit telling him that some people there that night needed freedom from self-hate. He was doing an altar call for anyone that wanted to be free from self-hate and thoughts of suicide. I knew 1000 percent that I wanted to be free from it, but I paused for a moment in fear of what the people that I came with would think. I began to have a panic attack. The Holy Spirit asked me, "Is what they think more important than the freedom you could have?" The answer was a clear *no*. I was over myself and what others might think of me. I was done with all the lies I had been told and took to heart. I needed to be free. I couldn't live another day feeling the way I did. I got up, put my focus on getting to that stage, and had to keep myself from running down there. So many other people in that room came that night that I ended up right against the stage. I closed my eyes, lifted my arms, and just surrendered it all to Jesus. No one laid their hands on me or anything. I was surrounded by people, but it was like it was just me and Jesus for a moment. I walked away literally feeling lighter. I was able to walk up straight with my head up instead of slouching, trying to nearly just disappear so no one would notice me. As mentioned, I have tried many drugs, the high from those drugs were nothing compared to the high I got from God that night. It lasted for days. He freed me from chains that bound me for nearly thirty years. I felt like a new person. It's been over two and half years since that night, and every time I think about it, I am in awe and feel so grateful that God made things work out.

I would be lying if I told you that sometimes those thoughts of self-hate don't try to come back and take hold of me. Now though my self-worth is anchored in my identity in Christ. I am his child, and no matter what, he loves and accepts me. God loved and accepted everyone from the beginning, even knowing what we all would do since he knows the beginning from the end. When he created us in his image, he said it was very good. Not just good, but very good.

I am here to tell you that no matter what you have been through, are going through, or will go through, God loves you and accepts you. He doesn't want you to be weighed down by burdens that aren't yours to be carried. He wants to free you right now. He wants you to hand it over to him. It is never too late for him to free you. It doesn't matter if you have been carrying it around for days or decades, he wants to free you from it today. What he has done for one person, he will do for another. That is why testimonies are so powerful because they are fulfillments of God's promises and they are to show others that he can and will do it for you too. Take hold of his promises!

> *Then Jesus said, "Come to me, all of you who are weary and carry heavy burdens, and I will give you rest. Take my yoke upon you. Let me teach you, because I am humble and gentle at heart, and you will find rest for your souls. For my yoke is easy to*

bear, and the burden I give you is light." (Matt. 11:28–30)

Then Peter replied, "I see very clearly that God shows no favoritism." (Acts 10:34)

Loss and Restoration

Parts of this chapter might be difficult for some to read. I am going to be graphic and not sugarcoat anything. It's the only way to truly convey what we went through.

As a typical little girl, I went through stages of playing mommy and wanting to have kids. As I got older, I still had a desire to be a mom but was concerned if I would be good at it.

As a teen, I had concerns if I even would be able to have kids. My periods were never regular like all the textbooks and such say they should be. Also, I had an irregular Pap smear when I was around fifteen or sixteen. I believe that came back with abnormal cells on my cervix. The doctor had to do cryotherapy to remove them. It was a very unpleasant procedure. My parents also made me get on Depo-Provera birth control because of my boyfriend at the time, which I talked about in the "Self-Worth" chapter. This made me not have a period for over a year, and I gained an excessive amount of weight quickly. My periods, when they came back, were worse than before.

Because my periods were so irregular, there were a few times that I thought I might be pregnant. I would be like 90 percent scared and about 10 percent excited until I found out I wasn't. I was mostly scared because I knew I wasn't ready or with the right guy to get support. I was excited because part of me wanted to be a mom and was unsure I would ever find the right guy.

Jump forward a few years, and I was finally with the right guy. At the beginning of our relationship, we both agreed we weren't going to have kids. At the time, I was okay with that.

In 2004, my periods started getting much heavier. July ended up being the climax of them, and it nearly killed me. On a Thursday, the bleeding started. I went through way too many pads. Friday morning, Curtis had gone to a store that was about twenty minutes away to get more pads and some Propel water for me to drink because at that time I was such a picky drinker. I wouldn't drink plain water. While he was gone, I went in the bathroom to change my pad yet again because it was overflowing. One moment I was on the toilet, and then the next, I woke up lying on the floor in pain. I had passed out for an undetermined amount of time. Thank God, I didn't land in the cat litter box that was also in there or hit my head on the tub or anything. Once I was able to get up and clean up to go back in the bedroom, I called Curtis frantically. I was quite shaken by the incident. I had never passed out like that before. I told him he needed to hurry home and take me to the hospital. Saying I wanted to go to the hospital was a huge deal. I absolutely could not stand to go to hospitals.

The weather that day was stormy, and the drive to the hospital was about twenty plus minutes. On the drive, I started having a panic attack about going to the hospital. We didn't have insurance, and I didn't want to deal with doctors or tests. We pulled up into the parking lot. Curtis was trying to convince me to go inside when the whole building went dark because they lost power. I told him that was a sign that we should not go there. He knew he couldn't change my mind, so we drove to a friend's apartment not far from the hospital just in case. We hung out there for hours before going home.

At this point, I was pale, had a hard time catching my breath, and was weak. I barely slept at all that night. I couldn't even lie down in the bed. I was sitting up in my computer chair. I honestly felt like I was dying, and the blood was showing no signs of slowing down.

Saturday, I was so pale you couldn't even see the lines in my hand. The fatigue was so bad. Curtis had to help me walk. My heart felt like it was going to pound out of my chest, and I finally gave into Curtis's demands to take me to the hospital. This time he drove us to a university hospital that was forty-five minutes away. We got into the emergency room, and like expected, it was crowded. We quietly filled out the forms and waited for our turn. We hadn't been there long and they hadn't taken anyone back yet when the triage nurse comes out to look at all the patient cards to call the next person back. She looked straight at me, then started flipping through all the cards and called my name. Several others in the waiting room that had obviously been there much longer than us were not too happy about that.

She did the normal vital checks and asked what the problem was. I explained to her that I was having an extremely heavy period, that I passed out, and felt awful. I was zoning in and out of reality. She got us a room and hooked me up the pulse and blood pressure monitors. I remember seeing my pulse fluctuating between one hundred and one hundred sixty. The resident doctor came in and asked me what's wrong. I explain everything to him. He then rudely told me I shouldn't have come to the ER and that I should have just waited till Monday to see a gynecologist. Because I had, he was obligated to run some blood tests, which included drug tests and a blood count. That was the last I saw of that doctor. Curtis and I were hopeful that he felt like a jerk and realized how wrong he was for treating me the way he did when the blood count came back. I was at a six when it was supposed to be thirteen. I was severely anemic. I had several nurses come in my ER room randomly to just see me because they hadn't seen someone with that low of a blood count being conscious. My skin was so pale it was almost translucent.

I was admitted into the hospital and given a blood transfusion. They also gave me a pill that was supposed to stop the bleeding, but God had already done that. While I didn't have a relationship with God at this time in my life, I still believed in him and that he could heal. Curtis did have a relationship with God, and even if he never said a prayer out loud, I know he had been praying for me. God had much bigger plans for me. Thankfully, my story didn't end there.

I did end up going to a gynecologist after being released from the hospital. More tests were run, but none ever showed the cause as to why I nearly died. My blood count went back up to thirteen, and the doctor put me on birth control pills to try to regulate my periods. They only worked for a few months before my periods went wonky again. No one, including myself, could stand who I was when on medication, so I stopped taking them. I went back to irregular periods but never had that much bleeding again, thank God.

In April 2007, the subject of having kids came back up. After much discussion, we decided that we would have a child. Being the planner that I am, we picked out names one for a girl and one for a boy.

Four months later, at the end of August 2007, I excitedly got my first positive pregnancy test. I took several different kinds to make sure. A couple of weeks later I was able to go to the health clinic to be tested. The doctor told me it was negative, that I wasn't pregnant. Even though the doctor refused to say I had a miscarriage, I know in my heart that is exactly what it was. I started bleeding right after the appointment. My heart was crushed, but I knew I could get pregnant at least. We decided to continue on trying.

Years went by, and in May 2009, my period started, but it didn't stop. It wasn't that heavy; it was just constant. I would have a day or two here and there with no blood, but that's it. This went on for over a year. Every time I hear the story in the Bible about the woman who bled for twelve years, who was so desperate for it to stop that she pushed through the crowd just to touch Jesus's hem, I could feel her pain. I know her situation was way worse because of the time and that it went eleven years longer, but I was so desperate for it to stop. I was sick of bleeding and had such a longing on my heart to have a child. That obviously couldn't happen when I was bleeding.

On May 25, 2010, I felt this urging that I should give up soda. It was a big deal for me because as I said previously, I am picky about food and drinks. Soda was 90 percent of what I drank. Exactly thirty days after I stopped drinking soda, the bleeding stopped and I returned to having normal, for me, periods.

I had many moments over the years of trying to conceive. When I saw others getting pregnant and having children with no issues but didn't even want kids, parents that don't even take care of the kids they got blessed with, it hurt my heart. Why them and not me? I wanted to have a child so much, yet I was denied. I would think also when it is finally my turn to have a child, that child would be spoiled. I mean how could I not spoil the child I had desired for so long?

One Sunday before church I actually had a discussion with someone about spoiling my child, and no joke, that day the pastor talked on that exact subject. It was our responsibility, given by God, to raise the child to understand morality, authority, rules, consequences to one's actions, and know the love God has for them. If they don't learn to follow instructions you give as their parent, someone they can see, then how will they follow the instructions of God who they can't see. I knew that message was for me. The Holy Spirit really opened my eyes on that subject that day. I would have to find the balance. It's okay to spoil a child now and then with special treats, gifts, or adventures; but the child also needs to be disciplined. I would like to point out discipline isn't beating your child into submission. Discipline doesn't even have to be physical. Am I against spanking a child? No, I believe under certain conditions it's okay. However, it should not harm the child.

> *Those who spare the rod of discipline hate their children. Those who love their children care enough to discipline them. (Prov. 13:24)*

> *Direct your children onto the right path, and when they are older, they will not leave it. (Prov. 22:6)*

In January 2011, the new associate pastor at our church, Shawn, recommended that the church start the new year with twenty-one days of prayer and fasting. I decided to join in, and one of the main things I was praying for was having a child. On January 24, 2011, during the fast, I was having normal random dreams when suddenly everything changed. I got this sensation that this was not a dream to me. It didn't even feel like a dream, more like a vision. Some may say they are the same thing, but for me, it was completely different.

I was shown this arcade-style game where you put quarters into play. The game itself wasn't important. I immediately focused on the quarter slot. A quarter was inserted into the slot; but instead of taking it, it was ejected, along with a second quarter. Instantly, the two quarters were lying flat next to each other with a white backdrop. The image zoomed out from the two quarters to five quarters. The quarters transformed into five human head silhouettes. The one on the far left was Curtis; next was me; and the last three were young kids, which at the time I guessed were boys because of the short hair. It appeared that they were in order of age. The first two kids were the same height, and the last was smaller. I woke up with an urgency that I needed to remember what I had seen.

At first, I questioned what I had just experienced, wondering if it was my overimaginative mind and my strong desire to have kids. At this point, it had been almost four years that Curtis and I had been trying. I remember even asking God for another sign to prove it was him that gave me the vision. Afterward, I felt it was wrong. I was being just like the Israelites, always wanting God to prove himself. I had my answer already because it was like nothing I had ever experienced before. Not to mention, I never thought about having three kids. I just thought having one healthy child would be enough. And if I was really blessed, we would have one boy and one girl.

I tried going back to sleep but was a bit overanxious. Again, the planner in me started trying to think of more names. While thinking of possible names, I clearly heard Nathanael Thomas said in an assertive tone. I lay there wondering why that name. When picking out names originally, the name Nathanael was one I had looked up the meaning to but didn't remember at the time. I never looked up Thomas because it's my dad's name and never planned on using names from my family. I did eventually get more sleep, and when we woke up, I told Curtis.

Later that afternoon, I got on the computer to look up the names. *Nathanael* means "God has given." I was okay. It made total sense. When I looked up *Thomas*, I may have screamed a little and almost fell out of my chair. *Thomas* means "twin." At that moment I got so excited and had absolutely no doubt that the vision was from God. Being the awesome God he is, he gave me the second sign I asked for.

At the time, I only shared that vision with a few people I trusted. I could tell they were hopeful for me but had their doubts. I tried not to let that affect me.

On May 8, 2011, the morning of Mother's Day, I felt the urge to take a pregnancy test before church and was ecstatic to see it say "*Pregnant*." When we went to church, they were doing a Mother's Day thing and I couldn't keep my excitement contained and told everyone. They all had been praying with us, so it seemed right. I announced it on Facebook by changing my profile to a photo of the pregnancy test and posting the following scripture because it was one I meditated on constantly.

> *He gives the childless woman a family, making her a happy mother. Praise the Lord! (Ps. 113:9)*

Two days later, I was able to have an ultrasound done and see the little baby and hear the heartbeat. My estimated due date at that time was December 31.

Two days after the ultrasound, on May 12, I get the news from my mom telling me that her mom (my Nana) passed away. While I was happy to be pregnant finally and to hear that my Nana did get to find out that I was pregnant, I was sad to have lost her. She lived in New Jersey, so we didn't get to see her much, and Curtis never got to meet her, but he did get to talk to her at least.

Because of Medicaid issues and a busy doctor's office, my first appointment wasn't until July 18. The office I was going to was about forty-five minutes to an hour away from the house. Curtis was able to get the day off though to go with me. We got there, and after waiting over an hour in the waiting room, we found out they were only having me fill out paperwork that day and I had to go back four days later to have an exam and ultrasound done.

Four days later, I was alone. Curtis was out of town, working. I drove down to the doctor; parked in the big parking garage; and waited in the waiting room, which was crowded. People were constantly in and out. After about an hour, I finally got called. They did the ultrasound first. It was amazing to see my baby and find out it was a boy. I felt a little disappointed Curtis missed out. They sent me back into the waiting room to wait another thirty-plus minutes before being called back again, this time to an exam room.

I waited in there for a while before the doctor and a student came in. They said the ultrasound looked good and did an exam. The doctor let the student do the exam, which I had no issue with. He said something didn't feel right and wanted the doctor to check it. She checked it and said she would like a transvaginal ultrasound done. They had me get dressed and go over to the ultrasound room again.

This time I had to get undressed, and a lady did the exam but wouldn't talk to me. When she finished, she said, "Wait here, I will get the doctor." I was sitting on the exam table half naked, worried about what's going on, and alone for over thirty minutes before the tech showed up again. She was surprised to see me. She asked if anyone had come in, and I said no. She told me to go ahead and get dressed and she would get someone. I did as she said and continued to wait for about another thirty minutes. I was getting more and more anxious as time went by, trying not to have a full-on panic attack. By the time the tech came back again, it was getting close to five o'clock. I had been there for half the day, and they were about to close. She was again surprised to see me and told me to follow her. She placed me in an exam room and left the door open.

I was sitting there waiting and my mind racing on what could be going on. When the doctor that first saw me walked by the room and saw me, she had this expression on her face like, "Oh, crap." She walked to the door and asked why I was still there. I told her I was told to wait for the doctor. She then said, "Oh, the other doctor didn't come talk to you?" I told her no. I could tell she didn't want to have to talk to me, which freaked me out even more. What was so bad that the doctor didn't want to talk to me and tried to pawn me off to another doctor? She then came in the room and told me my cervix was at four millimeters thick instead of the four centimeters that it was supposed to be at seventeen weeks pregnant. Then she proceeded to tell me that I would probably lose the baby soon and that I should go walk over to the hospital to be admitted in labor and delivery. Then she left. The hospital was on the other side of the huge parking garage. It freaked me out. Here I was all alone and had been here for hours now, almost everyone else was gone, and got told, with little to no compassion, that I was going to lose my baby boy. I was in tears as I left, and I still had to check out. I made it to my car in the parking garage before I had a full-on breakdown.

My cell phone only had enough minutes on it to make one phone call. I tried to compose myself to call Curtis to tell him what happened, but honestly, I was pretty hysterical. Thankfully, he had just got back in town. His work let him borrow a vehicle to come to me. It was going to be an hour before he arrived, so I waited in my hot car, praying and texting a few people who I knew had faith for a miracle.

We walked over to the hospital when he finally arrived and headed toward labor and delivery. We explained what the doctor told me, and they put me in the observation area until they could run tests of their own. I was admitted after the tests and put in an inclined bed (feet up in the air) to keep pressure off the cervix to try to save the pregnancy. They wanted to do a cervical cerclage, but Curtis and I prayed and decided it wasn't the right thing to do. After spending the weekend in the hospital with no signs of labor, I was sent home on strict bed rest.

Strict bed rest was no fun, but I learned to deal. Curtis helped out a lot and attempted to cook for me. A week later I went to the doctor again. The baby was looking good, and they made me do the one-hour glucose test. I didn't see how that made sense personally because I was supposed to be on strict bed rest, but they wanted me to sit/stand around for over an hour after already being out of bed for already two-plus hours going to the doctor.

Another week passed. It was now August 5, and my dad came over to bring some pasta and peas that my mom made me. I had been craving it. He stayed awhile and socialized with me, which was really nice because even though I tend to be antisocial by nature, I was missing some face-to-face talking. I had been getting more cramps during the day than before, but I thought it was just being in bed and not doing anything. I recall having some odd discharge, but at the time, I didn't think much of it.

We went to bed like any other night, but a little after midnight on August 6, 2011, I woke up feeling like I really had to poop. I got on the toilet and something didn't feel right. It felt like something boney going down and coming out my vagina. I was positive I felt our baby boy Malachi Zeke come out. I screamed for Curtis. I couldn't bring myself to look in the toilet to verify. He woke up and rushed to the bathroom to see what was wrong. I explained to him what I believe happened, and he looked in the toilet that I was still sitting on. He verified what I thought was true and said the cord was hanging, meaning the placenta had not yet come out. He didn't tell me at the time, knowing I couldn't have handled it in that moment, but when he saw our little Malachi, he was alive. I was only nineteen and a half weeks along, which meant it was impossible for him to survive because his lungs were not developed enough. I sat there on the toilet for a while with Curtis next to me waiting for the placenta to come out because that's what we thought we were supposed to do. We had heard of several stories of home births/miscarriages that didn't need any intervention.

In the time we were waiting, there were a lot of tears and heartache. I had a moment of complete despair that I felt like if something like this could possibly happen again, I could not risk trying again because it was too emotionally painful. I felt like a little part of me died. I told Curtis that I didn't want to try to have kids anymore. He just looked at me held my hand and didn't say anything. He didn't have to because the Holy Spirit swiftly reminded me of the vision I had at the beginning of the year and that God is a God that keeps his promises. He would be faithful and fulfill the promise of us having children. I immediately declared out loud to the devil that he was a liar and that my God would get me through this and would give us children. I refused to give up! I would hold on to God's promises!

I sat there very uncomfortably for nearly an hour, but the placenta never came out. Curtis called my parents and told them what happened and asked for advice because we knew my mother would probably be up anyways. She was obviously upset about what happened and advised us to call the hospital. We called the hospital, and they said we needed to call 911 to have an ambulance come get me for transportation to the hospital. So we did, then waited twenty plus minutes for them to show up. They clamped off the umbilical cord and had me get in the ambulance. They bagged up our precious baby boy and brought him along. I never did have the nerve to look at him. I know while I had God strengthening me to get through it all, that I just couldn't bear it at the time. They would not let Curtis ride with me, so my anxiety level was even higher for the twenty-five-minute drive having to be with strangers and have no control over anything. I was so out of it at the time. I forgot to warn them that my veins don't like cooperating for normal-size adult IVs. So they tried a few times before giving up and deciding to let the hospital deal with it. They took us to the closer hospital versus the one I was in two weeks prior.

Once at the hospital, I immediately asked where my husband was, but they had to follow protocol, making sure what happened wasn't domestic violence. After a little bit, they let him in the room with me. My parents showed up later on. The doctor on call said they had two options. One is a D&C (dilation and curettage), which is very invasive, or they could induce me with drugs to make me go into labor to push out the placenta. I have heard from many others that had miscarriages that most doctors just want to do the D&C because they can quickly get it cleared out. This doctor, however, didn't want to do that. He wanted to do the induction. I was glad to hear that because I really did not want to have the other procedure done. I should mention at this point we hadn't actually met the doctor.

I took the pills they gave me and waited for them to take effect. After a while, the contractions started. The pain increased with each one. They gave me some medication for the physical pain. My emotional pain was something else. Knowing I was going to endure all this and not having a child to hold afterward was excruciating. The first time they had me push, they insisted everyone leave the room including Curtis. I was miserable. The placenta didn't come out the first round, only a lot of blood, so they gave it some more time before I had to try again. I was weakened by the ordeal. I had issues sitting up on my own. For the second round, I demanded that Curtis was allowed to stay. This time, with lots of blood, the placenta finally came out.

When the doctor finally arrived in person to talk to us, he had a chance to look at our little Malachi. He told us that many times when this happens, it's because of a defect in the baby, but from what he could see, Malachi was perfect. I was running a fever though, so he was going to admit me to the hospital to stay a couple of days to test for infection. He listened to us tell our history of trying to have kids, the first miscarriage, and how we were treated by the other doctor's office and hospital. He seemed to genuinely care, which was a little shocking to see after our previous experiences. He told us we were right to deny the cervical cerclage because not having a history of a weak cervix, it's not recommended. He decided to go ahead and run a bunch of other tests to see what might have happened since there was no obvious cause as to why I had two miscarriages.

I remember when I got wheeled from the emergency room to the hospital room that the nurse on the floor I was moved to saw blood on my foot and tried to lighten the mood by saying, "Did you get bit by an alligator?" I just shrugged my shoulders in response. She didn't hurt my feelings or anything, I was just exhausted and I could tell by the Spirit she had a good heart. When she came back later, after she was able to read my chart, she apologized. You could see how bad she felt. I told her it was okay, that it didn't bother me.

I felt like a human pincushion with all the blood work being done and having issues with the IV as they kept having to move it. By the time I got released, I had been poked over twenty-seven times. Yes, I was counting. Not much else to do at that time. I didn't have a smartphone then. I did end up having an infection. I was given antibiotics through the IV. My blood count was low, so I was also given a blood transfusion.

I couldn't stand the food there. Like I said before, I am a picky eater. Curtis's parents were visiting at the time, and Curtis and I got in a little bit of an argument about it. I pushed him away from me. Two seconds later, I told him to get back over and hold my hand because I was all over the place emotionally and my hormones were crazy too. When he grabbed my arm, he said, "You are really hot." I retorted with, "Well, duh, that's why you married me!" It was hilarious to see all three of their faces because I caught them completely off guard. His parents had the classic jaw-drop expression, and Curtis was in shock but happy to see me smile for the first time in a few days.

I was released from the hospital and had appointments scheduled to see a blood specialist and the obstetrician-gynecologist (ob-gyn) I met in the hospital. Even though the circumstances we went through were dreadful and God did not cause them, God did have some good come out of it all. It is doubtful we would have met the doctor that we had during the situation under any other circumstances. He remained my doctor throughout all the following events, and I am grateful God placed him in our lives for that season.

> *And we know that God causes everything to work together for the good of those who love God and are called according to his purpose for them. (Rom. 8:28)*

When I went to the hematologist, I was told that I had a protein s deficiency, which means that I could have blood-clotting issues. There was no reason to treat it at that time; however, if I got pregnant again, they would need to retest. That would determine if I needed a daily heparin shot. I was also still anemic, but my numbers were going up, so it was fine. During my checkup with the ob-gyn, he said I was healing correctly. In addition, my ovaries had plenty of eggs and that it wasn't a matter of if I could get pregnant again but when it would happen. Overall, all the news was good. We decided to pray for healing on the protein s and trust in God's timing.

Three days after starting my twenty-one-day fast in January 2012, I got a positive pregnancy test. On the twentieth of January, I had my first ob-gyn appointment. The baby looked good and was measuring five weeks. Because of my previous issues, the doctor wanted to see me two weeks later after some blood tests were done.

Praise God, at the next appointment, it showed that God healed my protein s deficiency so no shots were needed.

Late the next night, on Saturday, February 4, I had some really bad cramps followed by a large clump of blood that came out. We prayed and felt like we should just wait till Monday to call the doctor if nothing else happened. The rest of the weekend was uneventful. Monday, the doctor did another ultrasound, and I had a subchorionic bleed that moved the baby right over the cervix. This type of bleed normally resolves itself, and most go on to have healthy pregnancies. All we could do is pray that God would heal it and nothing else would happen.

Everything seemed like it was going good after that until March 20 when I got some extreme pain in my right hip area. It hurt so bad it made me vomit repeatedly. Curtis was working, so his mom came and took me to the doctor. The baby was fine, and the doctor thought it was sciatic nerve or a pulled muscle, so he gave me muscle relaxants and pain medicine. The pain lasted for five hours that day. The next night the excruciating pain started again and lasted for over seven hours. The medication didn't seem to help at all. The pain only went away for good when I read the Word of God/Bible for a while. I have found that many times over the years that when I am having pain and prayer and medication don't help, I go to God's Word. I would start reading and meditating on that, and then I would get relief. It doesn't even have to be specific scriptures on what I am dealing with. I seek the Holy Spirit on what I should read whether it be Psalms or something else. There are times I will also just randomly open my Bible and read wherever it opens up.

Minus normal pregnancy issues like morning sickness, which might I say is named wrong because it doesn't just happen in the morning, the pregnancy was going fine. There were no other issues until Saturday, April 21, around 5:00 p.m. I went to go potty when I felt like something was coming out of my vagina. I could feel a sac coming out. I screamed for Curtis. I couldn't believe this was happening again to us. Moments later my water broke. I was only eighteen weeks pregnant, which meant that there was no chance the baby could survive. We prayed about what we should do and decided to head to the hospital. We got to the emergency room and explained what happened. The resident doctor didn't believe I knew what I was talking about until they finally did the ultrasound and saw that the fluid was indeed gone. Our OB doctor was then called.

When he got there, he told us about the two options we had. First, we could wait to see if the sac sealed itself and if the pregnancy would go forward, or I could be induced to go ahead and give birth to our child who would not be able to survive. He left the room to give us time to decide. In my heart, I knew this pregnancy was not going to end with a happy ending at this point. The idea of dragging it on more was too much for me. While my heart was broken, I had a peace about it that only God could give. God had given me a promise, and he was a faithful God. Curtis agreed with my decision to go ahead and be induced.

The doctor said he would get me admitted into the hospital and get the process started. He was waiting for us in the room I was moved to, and he had a sad expression on his face. In the time it took them to get me admitted and moved, he made the decision that he just couldn't induce me. He didn't want me to wonder what if or feel guilty for my decision. He did want me to stay in the hospital for a couple of days for observation. While part of me wanted to hurry up and move on to healing, we agreed that we would give it some time.

It was a blessing to have a doctor that truly cared about me and my family. It reassured me God was working things for our good even if what we were going through at the time was agonizing.

Late Sunday night the contractions started all on their own with no medication. They gradually got more and more painful. I held out for as long as I could before allowing them to give me pain medication. I was given morphine since the baby wasn't going to survive, which made me quite sleepy. I was in and out of it all night. I went to the toilet to use it to potty, I thought; but instead, our little baby was born at 5:57 a.m. on April 23, 2012. Curtis got the nurses, who then clamped the cord and helped me get back to my bed. Then they took care of our child that was born alive. They asked if I wanted to hold the baby, but I just couldn't bring myself to do so. I did ask what the baby's gender was because at this point, we had never gotten to find out. I was informed it was a girl, and I made sure they knew her name was Safira Trinity. They asked one more time if I wanted to hold her before taking her to the nursery. After she was gone, they made sure that I delivered the placenta so I wouldn't have the issues I did last time.

Safira lived for a little over three hours, dying at 9:24 a.m. I was informed by the staff and a friend that went and saw her in the nursery that she was treated really well in that time. After she passed but before she was taken to the funeral home, I was peer pressured into holding her. They insisted that it would bring me better closure. Honestly, I don't believe it really changed anything except I was stuck with the image of my dead child in my head that I couldn't take home and watch grow up. Don't get me wrong, I understand that for some people it helps. I was given the blanket that was used on her, her hospital bracelet, a little pink teddy bear with the hat she wore, and some photos of her. I was treated for an infection and released the next day.

I carried around the little pink bear with the hat on for four days until our church gifted me with a silver bracelet with a heart charm that had "Safira Trinity" engraved on it. My parents blessed me with two more charms: one a smaller heart with footprints for my first loss and second a heart with Malachi Zeke. Grief is real, and everyone has their own ways of dealing with it. I don't believe in the saying time heals all wounds when it comes to grief. It has been eight and seven years since my babies went to be with Jesus, and the pain and tears still come at times. While writing this book, many tears have been shed, but I don't regret doing it. It's something that needs to be shared. People need to know they are not alone in their pain. Others have gone through similar things too, and it's the comfort and strength of God that gets us through it. I had two songs that helped me through the grief and still do. First is the bridge from "Give Me Faith" by Elevation Worship and "The Hurt and the Healer" by Mercy Me. I have listened to them probably hundreds of times because sometimes I just let it play on repeat. These are some scriptures I meditated on too.

> *All praise to God, the Father of our Lord Jesus Christ. God is our merciful Father and the source of all comfort. He comforts us in all our troubles so that we can comfort others. When they are troubled, we will be able to give them the same comfort God has given us. (2 Cor. 1:3–4)*

> *Each time he said, "My grace is all you need. My power works best in weakness." So now I am glad to boast about my weaknesses, so that the power of Christ can work through me. (2 Cor. 12:9)*

> *O Jacob, how can you say the* LORD *does not see your troubles? O Israel, how can you say God ignores your rights? Have you never heard? Have you never understood? The* LORD *is the everlasting God, the Creator of all the earth. He never grows weak or weary. No one can measure the depths of his understanding. He gives power to the weak and strength to the powerless. Even youths will become weak and tired, and young men will fall in exhaustion. But those who trust in the Lord will find new strength. They will soar high on wings like eagles. They will run and not grow weary. They will walk and not faint. (Isa. 40:27–31)*

Not only have I grieved for the loss of my babies, but I had a hard time dealing with the difference of how they were treated. God had to show me that it wasn't my fault, that we weren't as prepared the first time for what happened and we did the best we could with what we were dealt with. God didn't let them suffer, and they truly are in a better place with him.

Another thing that I had to deal with while grieving and recovering from losing Safira was that a week after giving birth to her, while sitting on the couch watching TV, I realized my shirt was all wet. No one had warned me that I could produce breast milk that long after I gave birth. Everything I had read was you would right away and if you don't breastfeed or pump, it would dry up quickly. While it was upsetting that it was just another reminder I didn't have my little girl there, God reminded me to look at the positive. Now I knew I could breastfeed. I hadn't been sure of it before since I heard larger breast women sometimes had issues.

On the one-year anniversary of Malachi's birth and death, I got a positive pregnancy test. We were so excited. When we told our family though that was not the response we got. Several literally said, "Again?" I won't lie, that hurt a lot, but I wasn't going to let them steal my joy. I had a promise from God, and he wasn't going to fail me.

At my first OB doctor's appointment, the doctor said he knows the test came back negative for protein s deficiency, but after what happen with Safira, he was thinking it would be good to treat for it anyways. He suggested doing the heparin shots, which would be a shot I would have to inject into my stomach daily. Not only did I not personally like that idea because I hate shots, but also I felt in the spirit it was too much. We ended up compromising with me taking a low dose of aspirin daily. Everything looked good, and my due date was showing for April 12, 2013.

On the morning of September 11, 2012, I was dealing with the first trimester fun of fatigue and was dragging about getting out of bed. It was a bit after 9:00 a.m. and I was lying in bed trying to motivate myself to get up when suddenly I hear a knock on my door that made me jump. See, at the time, we lived on ten acres in the country, and knock on doors were not a common occurrence. I peeked out my bedroom window to see a highway patrol car. I thought it was odd, but I got up went to the door wearing my green nightgown and without my glasses that allow me to see. I opened the door, and the conversation went like this:

TROOPER: Are you Stephanie Anderson?
ME: Yes.
TROOPER: What is your relation to Thomas Anderson?
ME: I am his daughter.
TROOPER: Can I please come in?

At that point, my heart sunk and scenarios started going through my head. But I did not expect to hear what I did next. When I let the officer in, he motioned for us to go sit on the couches. I asked him if it was okay if I got my glasses first so I could actually see. He nodded for me to do so. I went and got my glasses, then sat on the couch opposite of him. The next sentence out of his mouth put me in shock.

"I am sorry to inform you that your father was in a car accident this morning and he died from his injuries."

He asked if there was anyone I wanted to call, and I said no because I didn't even know how to process what he said. He continued to give me information. I remember mindlessly calling Curtis. He was six hours away working in Georgia. I felt bad for him because he could barely understand me by this time, I was sobbing uncontrollably. After a few tries, he was able to piece together what had happen. I knew he felt helpless at the time because he couldn't be there for me. When I hung up with him, the officer continued to give me more information. When he was done telling me everything pertaining to the accident and what needed to be done next, he informed me that he had tried to go over to my parents' house to notify them first but no one answered. I told him that they were for sure home and that they were probably still sleeping. I asked him to go back over there and try again. He said that I could do that, and I was like, "No, I can't. I am pregnant, and they all have been sick." All of a sudden, he was all like, "Do I need to call an ambulance for you?" I remember thinking how odd it was. I was obviously distraught, but two seconds ago he was telling me to drive down the road three miles to tell them myself and now he wanted to call me medical help. I was polite though and just told him no but begged him to go over there and not leave till they answered.

After he left, I texted Curtis, asking if there was any possible way for him to get back to me. I knew it was a long shot because he worked on a tower crew and they drove company vehicles together. He responded, telling me he was already working on it. I attempted to calm down enough to call my pastor because even though I didn't want anyone there but Curtis (since I hate crying in front of others), deep down I knew I shouldn't be alone and that if I could just call him he would do something. The second I tried to talk though I broke down again, and it took him a little bit to understand what I was saying. All I asked him to do was pray. That helped me focus on God and calm down for a bit. A few minutes later, I got a call-back saying people were on the way. I don't know if they realize how much it really meant to me that they all cared so much, but it meant more than words can express. I never realized how important having a good church family was until then. I mean, they all gave me support and love when I had my two miscarriages, but that pain was different. See, I am a 110 percent daddy's girl. If God hadn't given me the dad that he did, I can promise you, I probably would not be alive. I got a call from Curtis telling me he was on the way back and that the ladies from his office were on their way to see me. I was totally against that because I barely knew them, but he said they insisted since he was so far away.

The drive to my house from town, like I said earlier, was about twenty-five to thirty minutes. During that time alone, I did talk to my mom on the phone, which was an extra-hard conversation because we were both distraught. I also made a declaration to the devil and God. In a less-than-two-year span, I lost two babies, both my grandmothers, a cat, and now my dad. I was over death. I declared that I would be having this baby. This baby would be healthy with no problems, and this baby would grow up to be an amazing person for God. That the lying and stealing devil was not allowed near my pregnancy or family. I had enough death in my life, and there would be life!

Eventually, people started showing up. I did make sure to get dressed before anyone arrived. In the six hours it took my husband to get home, people would come and leave but there was always someone with me. They got me food to eat and even tried to help by doing some cleaning. I would say the cleaning was sweet, but if you go to someone else's house, can I say don't try to put things away if you don't know where they go. No lie, it took me months to find some items. It was good to have people there. I would stop crying long enough to share some of my favorite memories. For instance, my mom and dad got in an argument as my mom was serving dinner one night. It was one of those rare nights that we were having a London broil. See, we didn't have much money growing up, so we rarely got steak. In my mom's anger, she threw the steak at my dad. My dad was mostly a pacifist and didn't yell too much or anything. He was not one to waste a steak. He was a meat and potatoes man. Seriously, if you think I am picky, he was near impossible. Us kids would hide veggies in his mash potatoes to try to get him to eat them. My dad very calmly got up, picked up the steak, brushed it off, put it on the plate, and started cutting it. This, of course, just made my mom madder; but it was, and still is, hilarious to me because of his expressions and all.

One would have thought after nearly seven hours of crying I wouldn't have any tears left, but the second Curtis got there, he held me, and I just cried and cried. Many tears have been shed for my father since that day.

The next day was in some ways even harder for me to deal with. My mom was inconsolable, and the funeral home needed someone to go down there and identify the body. I was told we just had to bring a photo. My sister's boyfriend at the time, Curtis, and I went there. When we get there, we are informed that only a blood relative could identify the body. The body wasn't actually there; they had a photo from the morgue. I had absolutely no desire to see my dad in the condition he was in. It was bad enough that the day before one of the people at my house brought up a story on the accident, showing a photo of it, and it had the yellow tarp covering his body. It was brutal. The accident happened around 6:30 a.m. when it was dark and foggy. My dad had to drive an hour to work on the interstate highway. A semitruck with trailer had stopped in the lane of traffic on the highway where the speed limit was seventy. My dad always did five to ten over the posted speed. Because of the conditions, according to the police report, most likely my dad never saw the trailer. There were even questions to if the driver of the semi had his lights on. My dad hit the back of the truck going approximately seventy-eight miles per hour. He hit it so hard it tore his aorta and died instantly. Like I said though it was brutal, and I knew he would look awful. Thankfully, it was a black-and-white photo, but it was an image seared in my brain that I wish I never had to see.

Those first few weeks I had to meditate on scripture to get me through each day. Along with 2 Corinthians 1:3–4 I listed earlier, these were the scriptures I would read repeatedly:

> *The* Lord *is close to the brokenhearted; he rescues those whose spirits are crushed. (Ps. 34:18)*

> *Weeping may last through the night, but joy comes with the morning. (Ps. 30:5)*

> *My health may fail, and my spirit may grow weak, but God remains the strength of my heart; he is mine forever. (Ps. 73:26)*

> *God blesses those who mourn, for they will be comforted. (Matt. 5:4, NLT)*

On November 23, 2012, we hit an important milestone in the pregnancy as we hit twenty weeks, which is halfway through. Even more excitingly, it was the furthest we ever made it. I had no doubt that this pregnancy was different and we weren't going to lose this baby. I had a list of scriptures on the notes on my phone that every morning I would read before even getting out of bed. Along with Psalm 113:9, I have mentioned before here are just a few of them:

> *Children are a gift from the Lord; they are a reward from him. (Ps. 127:3)*

The LORD *will give you prosperity in the land*
he swore to your ancestors to give you, blessing you
with many children. (Deut. 28:11)

Then God blessed them and said, "Be fruitful
and multiply..." (Gen. 1:28)

The pregnancy was pretty uneventful for the most part. I had normal pregnancy issues like morning sickness, fatigue, calf cramps, heartburn, and so on. I was diagnosed with pregestational diabetes, but it was mild, and no treatment was needed. The baby was quite stubborn about showing the gender though. We didn't find out until almost twenty-eight weeks pregnant that we were going to have a girl. We decided on the name Abigail Grace. *Abigail* means "father's joy," which was just so fitting considering everything we had been through. Plus, if she was going to be anything like me, she would end up a daddy's girl too. *Grace* was the idea of a friend of mine, the name of the church we were part of at the time, and the meaning "God's unmerited mercy (favor)" was perfect.

A few weeks after finding out we were having a girl, Curtis's maternal grandmother passed away. She had been sick and suffering for a while. I didn't really know her. She wasn't as social as his paternal grandma, but I still felt really sad for the family.

By thirty-seven weeks pregnant, I was beyond ecstatic to be full term. I was also beyond ready to have Abigail in my arms and not my belly anymore. I was more grateful than words can describe that we made it this far, but I was also quite uncomfortable. An interesting thing also did happen that I never expected. One day, randomly, at like eight o'clock at night, I got a call from my doctor. It concerned me at first, like why am I getting a call this late at night something has to be wrong. Nothing was wrong though, he called me because he was reading a magazine that was talking about blood clots in pregnancy and the use of heparin and thought of me. He told me that it confirmed what he told us at the beginning that I should have been taking it. He was glad though that there had been no complications. Here is this doctor that has hundreds of patients yet still takes the time to care for his patients and even calls an individual patient when an article reminds him of them. I had never heard of that before in this day and age. For me, it was confirmation that God had our backs and was guiding us on the path we needed to be on.

I had been trying everything that would induce labor from walking to eating pineapple, but nothing was successful. On April 5, 2013, the doctor decided to try and start an induction because of my past issues, gestational diabetes, and high blood pressure. They used Cervidil to attempt to soften my cervix to help induce the labor. It sits on your cervix for up to eleven hours. I don't recall how many hours it was on exactly, but I remember the burning pain was getting worse by the minute. I hadn't been comfortable with the whole idea of forcing the labor even though I really wanted to see my baby girl. The timing just didn't feel right. I requested it be taken out, and it was a good thing I did. They found out that I had a yeast infection that was probably aggravated by the medication. They gave me different medication to treat the yeast infection and sent home.

On my official due date of April 12, my doctor joked that I had to be the only one who enjoyed pregnancy that I stopped the induction and wanted to wait for it to be natural. As I said before, I was extremely uncomfortable and would have loved to already given birth weeks ago. However, I had to have peace with what I did, and I did not have peace with that induction. My God is greater than any circumstance that I am faced with. He said the decision was up to me, but he could only let me go so far past my due date before he would have to do an induction again.

I remember walking up and down my driveway one night having Braxton-Hicks contractions, trying to induce natural labor and getting completely overwhelmed with fear and doubt. How was I going to go through labor and push this baby out? How could I raise a child? Would I even be a good mom? Of course, by this point in the pregnancy, it was too late to change my mind. Curtis tried to reassure me that with God on our side, we could get through anything. As it was, we had already been through so much. I knew it was true that God wouldn't leave or forsake us and would empower us to do so. At that time though, my self-worth wasn't where it should have been. I had no self-confidence in my abilities. You can watch videos, read books, and get all the advice from people you know about how having a child will be and raising that child will be; but in reality, nothing truly prepares you for it. Situations can be similar to others, but they are never exactly the same because we are all uniquely made. Our individualism and expectations cause slight to significant differences of how we get through situations. For me, I had my mind set on how my child birthing experience should happen. I was determined to have an all-natural birthing experience. My water was supposed to break on its own. I was going to deliver my child vaginally with no pain medication, especially not an epidural. I had enough back issues; I didn't need them messing around with my spine and making matters worse, which I had heard could happen. There was no way I was going to have a cesarean section either. I was so adamant that I refused to even watch the videos on it or read much about it. My hubby was always telling me, "It's fine to hope for the best, but it's good to be prepared for the worst." I did not take his advice on that. I was in the mindset that if I even started to think about anything other than what I wanted to happen, it would put doubt in my faith and bad things would happen. We live in a fallen world; bad things will happen. Sometimes they can be prevented; other times you have to just work with the circumstances you have been dealt with, relying on the Holy Spirit to guide you the best way through it.

I was admitted to the hospital at five o'clock on the morning of April 25, 2013, to be induced. The hospital ultrasound technician measured the baby at about eight pounds in weight. About five hours later, the doctor came in to break my water. The nurses then made four attempts to get an IV line going to administer the Pitocin to really get labor going. Hours went by, and the contractions got worse, which was expected, but my pain tolerance level was not what I wanted it to be. Despite being adamant that I was not getting an epidural, I ended up getting an epidural. It numbed the pain enough that I could tolerate, it but wasn't too strong. I could actually still move my legs and such. I think the worst part of the epidural for me at that point was having to have a catheter because the person that put it in had some issues and caused some damage that took a week to heal. After so many more hours, I was finally fully dilated and allowed to push. I pushed for hours in all different positions, but she just didn't want to come out.

Eighteen hours after my water had been broken, the decision was made by the doctor that he was going to have to perform an emergency C-section. The baby was distressed, and I tried my best. A vaginal birth was just not going to happen, and it wasn't safe to continue to try to have one. Once I was being prepped for surgery, I went into shock. I had not mentally prepared for this possibility. I had never had a broken bone or stitches in my life, let alone major surgery. I didn't know what was going to happen. Since the epidural hadn't fully taken, originally, I was concerned that I was going to be able to feel them cutting me open and such. Curtis wasn't allowed with me for most of the prep and until they went to cut me open. I didn't like feeling alone and helpless as they strapped me down on this little operating table that was set up like the cross that Christ was nailed too. They even strapped my arms out to the sides like him. I felt like I could possibly be making the ultimate sacrifice for my child. I know what I went through was truly nothing compared to what Christ went through, but it really does change your perspective on things when put in a situation like that. I was hyperventilating from the shock, praying in my head that God would work it all out. I was glad when they finally let Curtis in the room. I didn't feel any pain as they cut me open, but it was quite uncomfortable. I could feel them moving things around, and they seemed to struggle with what they were doing. After what seemed like an eternity, they finally got her out at 5:37 a.m. on April 26, 2013, one year and three days after we had lost Safira. The doctor later would tell me he had to deliver her like a breech baby, one limb at a time, even though she wasn't breeched. I could hear her cry, and it was so beautiful. They only showed her to me for a second before whisking her and Curtis out of the room. At that moment I got to see her, so much love came over me, and I recall seeing a scratch on her cheek and getting upset that she got cut. As the medical team worked on putting me back together, they were jokingly taking bets on how much she weighed. It took a while before the nurse finally called the operating room to announce that she weighed twelve pounds and nine ounces! She was nearly the weight of a three-month-old. She wasn't a record for the hospital, but most of the staff there hadn't ever seen that big of a newborn. The doctor told me later that he should have done the ultrasound himself because he would have never let me attempt a vaginal birth with a baby as big as she was. I blame Curtis for how big she was because he had apparently prayed to God not to give us too small of a baby because he was concerned he would break it. God fulfilled that prayer.

Once they finished putting me back together, they transferred me to a normal hospital bed and wheeled me back into my room. Curtis arrived to the room a few minutes later. He had been in the nursery with Abigail. I wanted to see her and hold her so bad. I had waited over six years; I didn't want to wait any longer. But she had some blood sugar issues, and they had to monitor her. They said in an hour I could see her. Curtis and I had both been up for over twenty-four hours by now and were exhausted. I couldn't rest though; I wanted my baby. Curtis tried to nap, but I woke him up after an hour to find out what was going on. He came back and said they were still monitoring and I had to wait. I was not being very patient at this point, honestly. I would let him rest for about another hour and then make him check again. Finally, four hours later, I was able to see and hold my precious baby girl for the first time. Words cannot describe how the moment felt for me. To have that miracle child in my arms was beyond incredible. I never wanted to let her go.

She ended up getting jaundice, which had to be treated by being under a blue light. They also thought she had an infection, but it was just a false positive. After a few days in the hospital, we were finally able to go home. Her going-home outfit was too small for her weight and length. We had been abundantly blessed by family, friends, and church family with clothes, diapers, and other supplies for her that we didn't have to worry about needing much to start with. There was such an abundance of items that we actually were able to pass on the blessings to others, especially the newborn-size diapers and clothes that she didn't fit into. Baby formula was the only thing we didn't have a supply of. I had tried multiple times to breastfeed and pump;

but she had issues latching on, I just wasn't producing enough, and I was having issues from the C-section. The devil tried to make me feel guilty about it, but after a month of trying, I was at peace about just letting her drink formula only. She was healthy and getting what she needed; that was what was important. It didn't make me less of a mom to use formula.

A few months after having Abby, I was at church one day working and my pastor called me in his office to listen to something on a DVD. He went to play the part he wanted me to hear, but it went further back than he had planned. After listening to the part he hadn't meant for me to listen to, I knew God wanted me to hear it. It talked about a couple that didn't want kids because they couldn't imagine having to share their love with someone else, as if it would be limited or not enough for another. Curtis and I at this point had been together for nearly thirteen years. It was just the two of us for so long that honestly even though I knew God put the desire in my heart to have children, it freaked me out. We have such an amazing relationship. It was amusing that before we had kids, most people when first meeting us had a hard time believing we had been together for so long because of the way we are together. They would think we were in the newlywed stage still. We have always just been real with each other and others since day one. We are who we are; there is no faking it. We love each other no matter what. Does that mean we agree on everything? That would be a big, fat *no*. But that's okay. We wouldn't be individuals if we did. I am not trying to brag here; I am trying to make a point. Because we are so good together and it had been just the two of us for so long, the enemy really tried to use that against me to cause me to have fear while I was pregnant. I worried about what it would do to our relationship having a child. Would we no longer be us? I wondered a few times if we made the wrong choice to have kids. Of course, it was too late then. I took my strength from the Lord knowing that it would work out, that he wouldn't put something on us that we couldn't overcome with him.

Now I look back and laugh at how dramatic I got at times and how foolish I was to let the fear take over as I did. We are stronger and closer than ever. I feel our love, God's love, flowing through us to this precious miracle child that I couldn't imagine not having now. Seeing Curtis with Abby gives me such amazing joy. There are just no words to really explain it. God designed love. Love isn't limited. It's abounding, never-ending. It cannot fail. There is more than enough love for everyone and then some. I encourage anyone that reads this, please don't let fear rule your life because if you do, you will miss out on the amazing and very *good* plans God has for you. Just trust him. His love for us is more than we can fathom.

I had not given up on the vision God gave me about having twins and a third child. Many didn't believe in the vision I had especially after I had Abigail, but I refused to let their negativity get to me. On December 2, 2013, I got a positive pregnancy test. We were so thrilled and trusted God to protect this pregnancy. We decided to have a little fun with the announcement this time. We were doing a tenth-wedding-anniversary vow renewal that I had already been working on a photo slideshow for. To surprise everyone, the last slide was the image of the pregnancy test saying, "Fifth pregnancy due August first." When the slideshow played and that slide came up, we heard a ton of gasps and cheers. It was a much better reaction than we had gotten from the last one.

I went to the doctor a couple weeks later, and only one baby showed, but I still believed in a miracle of twins. I thought perhaps it's hidden behind the other and that maybe it wouldn't even be seen till I delivered them. Sometimes we can be so focused on how something can only work out one way or have one meaning. We get such a narrow vision while fixating on a few pixels of an image that we miss out on the beauty of the whole image. A vision or even word from God can be interpreted different ways. What we think is the right way isn't always the interpretation that God had in mind. We have to remember to not be so narrow-minded and focused on our will but to seek his will.

In April 2014, we found out we were having a boy. Even though I still believed in twins, I knew that this little boy needed to use the name God gave me in my vision, Nathanael Thomas. We decided to not reveal the name though, just the first initial *N* when we did our thirty-seven-week maternity photo shoot.

For the most part, the pregnancy was uneventful until the last month. The last month the whole family seemed to be attacked. I ended up getting pink eye with really bad swelling and pain, Curtis got pink eye too except not as bad, Abigail got a double ear infection, and we all got some sort of nasty stomach bug. I also had some pretty bad swelling all over from the pregnancy itself at this point, which made life quite miserable. I kept reminding myself that the end result was worth everything we had been through.

A few weeks before my due date, baby boy was measuring around ten pounds. The doctor said there was no way we were trying natural. It was safer to do another C-section again. We had no control over what date was picked. The doctor called the hospital while we were in the office, and the hospital told him what day and time they could schedule it for. The date was August 6, 2014. The doctor told me to go into labor beforehand though because the baby was already so big. I was nervous at the idea of having to be cut open again that it wasn't until after the appointment and we were almost back to the vehicle that I realized what day was chosen. I couldn't believe that of all the days that could have been picked, it had to be that day. I knew God was making a point that he was a God of restoration. He was restoring what was taken from us. Three years exactly from the date we lost Malachi Zeke, we would be welcoming Nathanael Thomas into this world. He wasn't to actually replace our lost son, but it was a victory over the enemy.

We had to be at the hospital at 5:00 a.m. on of August 6, so we had to drop off Abigail to Curtis's parents house the night before. It was the first time she was going to be away from us overnight. When we got to the hospital, they started doing all the pre-operation procedures. Again, I was taken into an operating room without Curtis to be strapped into the same cross-style operation table. I was given a spinal block this time that would wear off after a few hours. The first time they poked my spine, something wasn't right, and they didn't get any fluid. That meant they had to do it a second time. Later on, I would realize that the mistake they did caused damage. My upper back will randomly go sort of numb but hurt at the same time. Back to the operating room, I was trying not to freak out and just kept praying in my head because while, yes, I am alone without Curtis for physical support, we are never truly alone. God is with us always. The technicians get the block in finally, then laid me down and strap me with arms out on the table. After a little bit, Curtis is allowed into the room and the doctor started the operation. He used a laser to cut me open, and the smell of burning flesh was horrific. They struggled to get our big boy out just as they had with Abigail. Nathanael Thomas was officially born at 8:36 a.m. They checked him over and worked on him some before showing him to me for a brief moment before rushing him and Curtis out of the room. The nurses seemed concerned, and it had me worried a little. There was nothing I could do being strapped down, but I prayed though as they finished working on me. I did end up puking while they were putting me back together, which was horrible since all I could do is put my head to the side so as not to choke on it.

Once they were done closing me, I was taken to a room where Curtis was waiting for me. I found out Nathanael was bigger than his sister, weighing thirteen pounds and ten ounces and was twenty-two and half inches long. He was having blood sugar and respiratory issues that were beyond the capabilities of the hospital we were in. He was going to have to be transferred to the larger university hospital over an hour away. After an hour or so, he was brought into my room in a transportation box all tubed up and strapped in. I wasn't even aloud to touch him, only look at him for a couple of minutes before they took him away. They weren't transferring me with him. I wasn't doing so well myself at the time. I was having a reaction to one of the medications they gave me, and it was causing me to not be able to keep anything down, and when I wasn't getting sick, I wasn't able to keep my eyes open. Curtis was by my side the entire time, being as supportive as he could be.

When I was more with it hours later, I was looking at the photos taken of Nathanael since that's all I had of him at the time. The Holy Spirit reminded me of something someone had told me when I was pregnant with Abigail. A friend had a dream of me holding a mostly bald baby and Curtis holding a baby with dark hair. Abigail was mostly bald with only a little light-colored hair when she was born, and Nathanael was born with dark-brown hair. What a reminder of God's goodness and promises.

The next day, during one of the calls Curtis made to the other hospital, we found out that Nathanael was finally breathing on his own. He was still having blood sugar issues though, so they were keeping him on IV. It was nerve-racking being so far away from him and not even having the chance to touch or hold him yet. I was feeling a little better and could get up and walk to the bathroom, but my pain was worse. We had been discussing the differences between the two births and realized that Nathanael probably had more respiratory issues because he hadn't got the benefits of attempting to go through the birth canal and having the fluid squeezed out of his lungs during the contractions. The blood sugar issue probably had to do with his size. Several hours later, we found out that he was eating really good, and if he kept improving, the IV would be able to be taken out and he could be moved to a lower level of NICU.

I got discharged from the hospital on August 8. We immediately drove down to the hospital that Nathanael was in. We had called before we drove and were told that most likely he would be discharged that day also. Curtis had to drop me off at the entrance because I couldn't walk very far. He also had to get one of the hospital wheelchairs to get me to the NICU. I was so relieved and delighted to be able to finally hold my son for the first time. He was so big compared to all the other babies in the unit, the nurses were calling him Thor. I was so ready to take him home, but in the time it took us to get there, Nathanael had some issues while he was feeding that his oxygen levels dropped. He was trying to eat too fast and forgetting to breathe. They insisted on keeping him for another night to make sure everything was fine and he was eating and breathing correctly. It hurt both physically and mentally to have to leave him there for another night. I was also really missing Abigail. We hadn't seen her since we dropped her off at her grandparents the night before Nathanael was born.

Three days after being born, Nathanael finally got to come home and his sister was brought home by her grandparents. We were finally a family of four together. I know some people will say that three days isn't that long of a time, but for us, in that moment, it felt quite longer.

Nathanael, who goes by Nate, turned six years old a few days ago. Both kids for the most part have been healthy with very little issues. While I was pregnant with both and after they were born, I have prayed over them constantly for good health and that they grow up to be amazing children of God. You might be wondering about the vision in January 2011. Did I give up on it? No, I learned, as I mentioned before, that sometimes the way we think something should work out isn't always the way it is supposed to be. When I posted comparison photos of when Abigail was born that Curtis took and then the one he took of Nathanael, several people commented on the fact they looked like twins. Regularly over the last six years, I have been asked by many people if they were twins. They are fifteen months apart and are close in size, and while each has their own looks, there is no denying they are related. It wasn't what I expected, but I wouldn't trade it for anything. I am grateful God blessed me with them. What about the third child? Honestly, I have no intentions of ever getting pregnant again because it was really rough on me and I really do not want to deal with the baby/toddler stages again. Does that mean we will never have another child? No, because there are always other options, such as adoption. Do we intend on adopting anytime soon? No. We are in no rush and know at this time it's not the right time. What the future holds I do not know. I know that the vision was real, and that anything is possible. I know my God has been with me through all the losses and the restoration.

Ministry

God has given each of you a gift from his great variety of spiritual gifts. Use them well to serve one another. (1 Pet. 4:10)

Therefore, go and make disciples of all the nations, baptizing them in the name of the Father and the Son and the Holy Spirit. (Matt. 28:19)

But my life is worth nothing to me unless I use it for finishing the work assigned me by the Lord Jesus—the work of telling others the Good News about the wonderful grace of God. (Act 20:24)

Their responsibility is to equip God's people to do his work and build up the church, the body of Christ. (Eph. 4:12)

The word *work* in Ephesians 4:12 is from the Greek word *diakonia*, which means "ministry, to be a servant, or to serve." Too many people, when they think of ministry, they only think of the fivefold ministry (apostles, prophets, evangelists, pastors, and teachers). They miss the part where those in the fivefold ministry are to equip all the other believers for ministry work. All believers are called to ministry. No position in ministry is more important than another. We are all important in our own ways. We are a complete body of Christ when each of us does what God has gifted us to do. A body can function without some parts, but it will not work as effectively and how God designed it without all the parts.

The human body has many parts, but the many parts make up one whole body. So it is with the body of Christ. Some of us are Jews, some are Gentiles, some are slaves, and some are free. But we have all been baptized into one body by one Spirit, and we all share the same Spirit.

Yes, the body has many different parts, not just one part. If the foot says, "I am not a part of the body because I am not a hand," that does not make it any less a part of the body. And if the ear says, "I am not part of the body because I am not an eye," would that make it any less a part of the body? If the whole body were an eye, how would you hear? Or if your whole body were an ear, how would you smell anything?

But our bodies have many parts, and God has put each part just where he wants it. How strange a body would be if it had only one part! Yes, there are many parts but only one body. The eye can never say to the hand, "I don't need you." The head can't say to the feet, "I don't need you." In fact, some parts of the body that seem to be weakest and least important are actually the most necessary. And the parts we regard as less honorable are those we clothe with the greatest care. So we carefully protect those parts that should not be seen, while the more honorable parts do not require this special care. So God has put the body together such that extra honor and care are given to those parts that have less dignity. This makes for harmony among the members, so that all the members care for each other. If one part suffers, all the parts suffer with it, and if one part is honored, all the parts are glad.

*All of you together are Christ's body, and each
of you is a part of it. (1 Cor. 12:12–27)*

We are to spread the gospel not by words alone but by our actions also. It is true that actions speak way louder than words at times. I didn't always understand all of this myself. I went through a process of learning as you will read in this chapter.

My journey with ministry started months after Curtis and I started going to church. We had been attending on Sundays and sometimes Wednesday nights also. In order to serve in the church we were attending, you had to go through a membership class and agree to certain things. Baptism was also a requirement. I hadn't been baptized that I could remember. Curtis was already baptized, but so that I wouldn't be by myself, he decided to be baptized also. After all that, since both of us had a background in computer tech, the church asked for our help with the media. We helped as much as we could, but the people over it were quite restrictive in what they would allow us to do. I did get to start learning video editing to make more worship videos for the services since they didn't have a live band to play.

When the new associate pastor Shawn came on one night, he was having an issue with his iPod. He heard we were techs, so he came up to me and said, "This isn't working, fix it." Then he walked away. I instantly did not like this man because we hadn't even been introduced and he didn't even say hi or anything. It was extremely rude. I had never even touched an iPod before, and I could have told him that if he had given me a chance. This was also way before I had a smartphone. Even so, it wasn't like I could just easily google it. I had to wait to get access to a computer and try to look it up. Despite not being a fan of him personally, I was intrigued by his preaching. Just like the head pastor of the church, he had a different way of preaching than I was used to. He was very raw and added personal stories to get his point across. He wanted more media done like video recording for YouTube and making CDs for people to be able to take the messages with them. I reveled in getting to advance my nerd tech and be creative and helpful. I didn't think of it at the time, but it was me using my gifts from God for ministry. While I wasn't the pastor or teacher, I helped create items to spread the message of the gospel and I helped people engage into worship with the videos I created.

Randomly, one day, the lead pastor talked to me about perhaps me learning to do the bookkeeping for the church. They already had some older ladies doing it, and I guess, he thought it might be good to bring someone younger in to learn. It was odd to me because it wasn't like I had a background in it. I agreed to think about it and see what it was about. Before that could happen though, some of the elders of the church were not fond of the changes Shawn was making and there was a split in the church. Shawn, along with several other people, decided to start their own church.

I remember seeing an announcement about it and giving information to a meeting at a restaurant to discuss the plan on Facebook. It was an open invitation to anyone to come and be part of the meeting. At this point, I still wasn't a fan of Shawn as a person, but I had this strong urging from the Holy Spirit to go the meeting. Curtis didn't have any checks about it, so we went. It was so awkward for us because mostly everyone there had known each other for a while and was friends with Shawn. I felt like they thought we were spies for the church and just trying to find out gossip basically. Many years later I would find out that I was right about that. They really did think that. It was not our intention at all. I was completely out of my comfort zone by going, but I had to do what I felt God was telling me to do. I was excited about the vision Shawn had for this new church and wanted to be part of it. I didn't feel like I fit in though, and we were unsure about leaving the other church.

As they began to launch the new church in February 2011, we helped whenever we could with what we could. They were having their meetings in a conference room of a hotel. We would go help set up chairs, Curtis would help with the sound equipment, and I would help with some of the computer tech. For the first month or two, we were going back and forth between the two churches. When we started helping, we had no intention of actually leaving the other church completely. The new church just needed more help, and actually, they let us help more. We got an email from the lead pastor of the other church asking our intentions and such. After much prayer and consideration, Curtis and I decided that God wanted us to be part of the new church. It was a hard decision because we loved everyone at the original church; however, we knew it wasn't fair dividing our attention between the two. We needed to focus and move forward with what we felt the Holy Spirit was leading us to do.

After having to set up and take down the church at the hotel for a few months, they were able to lease out a building where not only could they set up and leave it but could also expand the ministry to be more than just Sundays. Things went good for a while, then something happened in October 2011: the bookkeeper, some musicians, and other members left the church. Shawn asked if I could help teach his wife how to do the administrative work including bookkeeping. Mind you, the most business experience I had was years prior when I worked as a shift manager at Pizza Hut. I have from many years done our personal finances using Quicken though. His wife at the time wasn't really interested in doing any of it, and I ended up doing it myself. I learned everything as I went. At the time, I didn't have a secular job and enjoyed feeling like I had a purpose and could contribute.

After doing it for months, I was given the official title of secretary and bookkeeper. It was an unpaid position, and I was fine with that. Even after when they tried to get me to take a salary, I refused because doing the numbers, I knew how much the church had and it also felt like I was taking from God. It would be years later before God changed my perspective on that. I was doing a job. Even if it was for a ministry, it was still work. It wasn't just helping out on Sunday. I did work for the church nearly seven days a week. Besides from doing most of the administration work, I also handled a lot of the media work too. I filmed the service, edited the videos, created CDs/DVDs, and eventually ran the website plus social media. I loved what I did for the church and spreading the gospel, but I had bills to pay, and all the work I did for the church prevented me from being able to have a paying job.

Don't hesitate to accept hospitality, because those who work deserve their pay. (Luke 10:7)

When people work, their wages are not a gift,
but something they have earned. (Rom. 4:4)

Honestly, I had taken on way too much because I didn't know how to say no or ask for help when needed. I was completely out of balance between ministry and home life. Curtis and I got in several fights over the years about me putting family second to the ministry and not taking care of myself. If your family thinks that you think the church is more important than they are, something is seriously wrong and you are not doing it God's way. They will grow up hating the church instead of loving and following God. I knew that to be in balance, I needed to put God first, Curtis and the kids (my home ministry), and then the ministry of the church. I would be good for a while and then fall back into bad habits. Then I would start the process all over again. I kept being told how I was essential to the church and that they wouldn't know what to do without me. It felt good to be needed, but it wasn't a healthy place for me or the church. After serving at the church for five years, and even staying after a change of pastors, I came to the hard decision that I needed to step back from it all to let the church grow the way it needed to and also for me and my family's health. When I had started, we didn't have any kids, but when I left, I had two toddlers. The church went through a rebranding after the new pastor took over, and when we visit the area, we attend the church when we can. I love seeing all that God has done to grow it into an amazing place that the city needed.

Attending church without having to do anything was really weird and felt unnatural. I wanted to be helping out but knew that I had to take a break and figure things out. Shawn, who had left the church for his own sabbatical because of changes in his life, including moving back to the area he grew up, roughly three hours away, contacted me a few months later saying he was feeling led to plant a church in the location he was living. He told me he wanted me to pray about being part of it because he couldn't imagine doing it without me. The location was near the beaches, which immediately called out to me. I missed living within ten minutes from the beach. I told him I would discuss it with Curtis and we would come visit to see what the area was like since I remember the culture being different near the beaches. Curtis knew the area a little bit because his family had friends near there with a kid around his age, so he grew up visiting that area. It wasn't something we could take lightly. Most of our family all lived within forty-five minutes of the house we lived in, which we had a mortgage on. We didn't know that many people in the other area. Curtis had a decent-paying job at a Target warehouse, but it was really physically demanding on him. The kids were still small and had only lived in the one house. There was a lot to think and pray about. Another big thing is, we knew that things had to be different from last time we helped plant a church. I could not be overburdened with trying to do so much on my own. I couldn't have my family suffer again because of my poor management. Another important factor is if we did uproot our family to move in order to plant this church and I was going to be working full time on it, I would need to be compensated. I didn't expect to get paid the same as if I had a secular job, but I needed enough to at least cover most of our rent.

Several months later, we got to visit the area and I fell in love with it. Once we got so close, I could just feel a change in the atmosphere. The kids seemed to like the area too. After much discussion and such, we made the decision to try and make it happen. There were no Target warehouses that Curtis could transfer to, only stores, which would mean a serious pay cut. We looked into other job options also. It seemed like if you didn't live there already, you weren't even considered. We took our time initially looking into possible places to live and find jobs. Months went by, and Shawn started holding interest meetings for the church plant and getting things lined up to figure out a launch date. I did as much as I could from where we were living: filing paperwork, setting up social media, a website, designing all the literature, and so on. We decided not to tell any of our family about the decision to move to help plant the church until we had more concrete plans. We knew some of them wouldn't react the best way, and they didn't. It may have been better to give them more warning, but it was a lesson we learned the hard way.

There were actually a few lessons we unfortunately learned the hard way during this chapter of our life. We knew, and still know, without a doubt that God wanted us to move to the Space Coast. However, we also know we missed God's best in some of the choices we made to make it happen in our timing and not his. I have heard people say you can't miss God, and I don't agree obviously. God gave us all free will because he wanted us to have the ability to choose. We choose to worship him; we aren't forced to worship him or to do anything else. We can hear from God and not do what he tells us too. There are many scriptures that say that God told someone to do something and they didn't. Jeremiah chapters 42–43 is a prime example of missing God's best. He told them not to go to Egypt and to stay in Judah and he would take care of them, yet they did not listen. God isn't surprised by your actions either. He knows what you are going to do; however, it doesn't stop him from trying to convince you to do what's best. He also will work your mistakes for your good in the end just like Romans 8:28 says.

We moved in February 2017, and the church was launched Easter Day, April 16. Through God, I did a lot better managing my family and the ministry. I wasn't perfect, but I tried to not become overwhelmed completely. I got help when I needed help, and I learned to say no. Things went really well for months. Then issues started with some of the leaders and congregation of the church that escalated to the point that the church was nearly closed at the end of May 2018. Instead, there was a change of leadership with several leaders and congregation leaving. The leaders that took over said that they would do it for a temporary amount of time until God brought in the right pastor for the church. At the time, the main reason I stayed on was because I didn't feel God was saying that I should leave. I didn't really know the new leaders, but they did agree that my position would stay the same as administrator and bookkeeper and my salary would remain the same also.

The church went through a major transformation under the new leaders because they did things quite different than the prior pastor did. I did not agree with everything that was done, just like I never agreed with everything that was done previously. As long as I didn't have a check from the Holy Spirit about it, I was fine. In some ways, I had more freedom in my creativity in what I did; however, they were more rigid and micromanaged other parts. I got frustrated quite a bit with some of it and wanted to just walk away. I didn't say anything to anyone but Curtis. I figured I was probably just so used to doing it one way that it was a learning curve that I just needed to deal with. I was asked to share testimonies in front of everyone, which was completely out of my comfort zone. I am a behind-the-scenes type of person, not a public speaker. Despite that, I do love sharing how awesome God is, and if my testimony can help someone else out, it's worth it.

A year went by, and things were going fine. I had a good balance between doing things for the church and home life. My family's world got turned upside down the morning of Friday, July 5, 2019. We had celebrated Fourth of July at a friend's house. We went to bed around 3:00 a.m. because we were on a night-shift schedule and normally wake up around noonish. On this day though, I got woken up around 9:45 a.m. by a horrible sound. I turned over in bed, and Curtis was lying on his stomach. His body became stiff, and he started to have a seizure. I freaked out but immediately laid hands on him and started praying. After about two minutes, the seizure stopped. He wasn't breathing right, his lips had turned blue, and was unresponsive to me. He was still kind of stiff too. I tried to wake him up, even told him that if he didn't respond I was going to have to call 911. He didn't respond, so I went got my phone to call. I was so frantic that I literally forgot how to use my phone and dial 911 for a minute. I asked God to help me calm down. I called and told them what happened. They said help was being sent and hung up. I always thought they stayed on the line till help arrived. I was at a loss. I tried calling the head lead couple of the church, but they didn't answer. I tried someone else, and they didn't answer. Finally, I got through to someone that I didn't know when I called but actually had experience with dealing with someone with seizures. He was able to reassure me that it was normal for the person to be unresponsive after a seizure. It's amazing how while God does not cause the bad to happen, he does help provide what you need to get through what comes against you. I was so grateful God put this person in our lives at the right time and that he was the one that answered the phone when I needed someone. The paramedics arrived, checked Curtis over, and started an IV. He fought them a little about this but not consciously as he still hadn't actually woken up. I will never forget the sight of them having to carry his limp body through the house to the gurney and then out to the ambulance. The second they left, I broke down. The kids were scared and didn't understand what was happening either because they woke up to strange people in the house and Daddy being carried out. I called Shawn and told him through the tears what happened. He prayed for us and talked to me until I calmed down. He was over three hours away; otherwise, he would have probably come to us.

It was about five to ten minutes after the ambulance left before the kids and I headed to the hospital because I had to be okay enough to drive safely. Thankfully, the hospital was only about five minutes from the house. We got there, and I told the desk who I was. They let us go see him. Curtis was lying in the hospital bed really pale and not conscious. I put my hand on his chest. I didn't verbally say anything to start with. In my heart, I was asking God to let my husband and best friend to be okay and not let me lose him. Curtis woke up seconds later with a confused look on his face. I told him what happened, and he was shocked. Curtis would tell me months later that the moment I touched him, it was like I pulled him back from somewhere. He says that, through God, I resurrected him. He didn't have details as to where, but he hadn't been in his body anymore. I was already thankful at the time he was still with us; however, when he told me that, I was beyond thankful to God that he gave my husband back to me. Not everyone gets that fortunate.

The first person I had talked to after the seizure came to visit us in the emergency room and was even nice enough to bring me and the kids lunch because we hadn't had a chance to eat. Honestly, it was the first time since Shawn left that I felt like I had a pastor again. He shared some information, read some scripture, and prayed over us before he had to head back to his job. See, while we had the head lead couple of the church, they weren't pastors to me. They specifically have even had said many times that they were not pastors. It was not the calling on their lives.

After the hospital ran tests and the results showed nothing wrong, they sent us home. I was shocked by this: a forty-year-old healthy male had his first random seizure with no indication of why and they only do just a couple of tests and send him home. Roughly four hours and ten minutes after his first seizure, we were sitting in our living room with the head lead couple of the church. Curtis was talking when all of a sudden, he starts smacking his lips together, did a weird laugh, turned his head off to one side, and started having a seizure. This seizure did not look like the last and lasted way longer. The kids were in the room when it started. I called 911 again while the couple started praying for him and helped get him on his side. This time the dispatcher stayed on the phone with me till the EMTs showed up. Curtis stopped breathing for about a minute, which completely freaked me out. The EMTs did not understand why the hospital would release him that quickly without any indication of what was going on. He was taken back to the same hospital, but they had no neurologist on call, which was my guess part of the reason they sent him home earlier. So he had to be transferred to another hospital to be watched overnight and given antiseizure medications. The lead couple agreed to watch our kids overnight so I could stay the night with Curtis at the hospital. He was so out of it and mostly slept. He couldn't remember coming home the night before and didn't even remember coming home from the first hospital. It was a long night, but thank God no more seizures.

We went home Saturday afternoon with a prescription and information to call and make an appointment with a neurologist. Our kids were brought to us that night, and they were happy to see Daddy home. Despite having slept most of the day before, he was quite fatigued and extremely sore. By Sunday, he was still having issues with fatigue, soreness, and feeling out of it; but we drove the forty-five minutes to church anyways. We both thought it would be good for us and the kids. It did exhaust him even more, and the long drive did not help at all either, but being in the house of God felt right.

Right before the seizures happened, the leadership in the church all agreed to have the person I mentioned that felt like a pastor to me during the event and his wife become the lead of the church. Several of us in leadership had heard from the Holy Spirit months to a year prior, when they first came to the church, and shared that they would be key leaders of the church. I do not know exactly what happened, but while I was dealing with my family's health issues, things took a turn at the church. From the information I was given, the head leaders that were supposed to hand over the leadership decided to really micromanage. They didn't like the new vision for the church, or the fact that things would change. It basically felt like they wanted things to stay the same except for who was officially leading. It made no sense to me because when they came in to start with, they made a ton of changes themselves. This is because each leader is different as we are uniquely made and have different assignments by God. I could not handle all the drama of the church on top of trying to take care of my husband that was not doing well at all. I did not go to several meetings because I put my family over the ministry like I needed too.

I got ambushed by the head lead couple one day. They were waiting at my home for me after I took Curtis to work. At this point, all other leadership in the church had left. As I said to them that day, there were wrongs done by everyone involved including me. If I am being completely honest, I had the choice to leave the church right then and I should have. I let fear take over because I knew we could not make it on Curtis's pay alone, especially since at this point he was struggling even getting out of bed some days and missing a lot of work. Some days were so bad that he couldn't even walk; he would crawl around the house. I agreed to stay though and was told that changes would be made, such as an actual vision for the church be established because they had the tagline "Reaching the Lost and Equipping the Saints." But they really didn't share the vision of how the church would do that and what the church planned for the future and also that they would get leaders, because at this point, it was down to them and me. That's not how to run a good church. I prayed for the best to come from the situation.

Months went by, and Curtis's health was still hit or miss each day. Things at the church did not change. I was changing though and not for the good. I was getting numbness and a hard heart to the church. It was no longer "I get to go to church" but "I have to go to church." If I could come up with an excuse not to go, I would. I could not stand to be there. I tried to engage in worship and all, but I just had this spirit of oppression and dread while I was there. Also, there was a lot of things done that felt forced and not a move of the Holy Spirit, and I just did not agree with it. Now hear me out, I am not judging the church or leaders; I am just stating my point of view. There were several there that enjoyed the church and did get some good from it. The leaders had good hearts, and I love them, but they weren't spiritual leaders to me and my family. Plus, it was a burden at this point to have to travel back and forth the way we were.

In October, I decided it was time for us to go. Curtis and I discussed the issues that might happen if I lost the pay, but we were willing to deal with the consequences. We arranged a proper meeting to discuss it with them. Fear took over in the meeting on both sides. They didn't say so, but it was obvious they were worried about losing me since they didn't have as much knowledge to running the church as I did. My fear was losing the pay. They made a suggestion of me cutting back my load and that we also didn't have to physically attend the church every Sunday. The way I was paid was changed to be a little less costly on the church. Curtis and I agreed to the terms.

The next couple months things did not get better; they got worse in fact. I came to the realization that I could not let the fear of lost income control me anymore. I always said God was my provider, but I still was trying to be in control. I was in a bad place spiritually, and it was affecting my health so much I had to get on blood pressure medication. My family was suffering from me being in a bad place also.

On January 5, 2020, the kids woke up around 11:30 a.m. and said they wanted to go to church. We couldn't attend the church we were going to as the service would be over by the time we got there. Plus Curtis was not able to get up yet. I looked up a church that was recommended to me that was only five minutes away. They were supposed to have a noon service, but for the new year, they changed their service times. They no longer had a noon service but now had a 5:30 p.m. It was perfect because it would allow Curtis time to wake up and be able to go with us.

The second I walked in, I felt at home and like a weight was lifted off me. Shawn had put this vision in my head over the years of the church he had wanted to build with the two church plants we did, and this church was like seeing that vision fulfilled. The pastor of the church even reminded me of Shawn with his raw and real message. The kids loved it, and when we left, they even asked if we could go back. I was refreshed during worship, and the message nearly screamed at me at what we as a family needed to do. Enough was enough. We had to fully trust God as our source. Fear would not have hold anymore. We needed to leave the church I was working for.

A couple days later I also ended up having a good conversation with Shawn, who I still consider my pastor, about everything. What he shared confirmed to me that we were doing the right thing. Before talking to him, I had a peace I hadn't had in a while, and afterward, it was even stronger. I wrote up a list of everything I did for the church, gathered together all information and resources I had, and sent it with a formal email telling them our decision to leave the church fully. I even gave them a month notice versus just the standard two-week notice.

I was excited to go to church again. I was back to "I get to go to church," not "I have to go to church." The only strange part was, I had attended church so long with almost always having to do something that it felt odd to get to just enjoy service. I ended up getting out of my comfort zone also and joining a small group that I knew no one in. It was based from the book *Lead like Jesus*. If you haven't read the book, I recommend it. It opened up my perspective on leadership and ministry. It also awakened passions/desires in me that honestly I had given up on long ago. During one of the exercises in it, the Holy Spirit reminded me of my desire to write a book. He then gave me the idea and title for this book you are reading right now. The COVID-19 pandemic started partway through the group, but we continued over Zoom. I was a little sad when the small-group semester ended but was grateful for the time I got in the group.

I had mentioned to someone that even after months sometimes it still felt odd not to have to do anything during church service, and they said, "Who knows what God will do one day soon, and you can be using your gifts in church again." It sparked something in me that too many look at ministry as what is done for the church-building services. Church isn't a building; it's the people. Ministry is doing God's work when and wherever he calls you to do so. While I wasn't serving at the church I attended, it didn't mean I wasn't doing things for the church. Technically, the blogs and testimonies I wrote, Shawn's writings I shared over the different social media platforms, and every other way I have shared the goodness of God and his gospel is all ministry. Serving at a church is a good form of ministry, but always remember ministry is way more than just that. Do as Matthew 28:19 says in the way God has gifted you to do so!

Holy Spirit and Blessings

In this final chapter, I will start out by sharing what I have learned about the Holy Spirit that I have mentioned numerous times throughout this book and will end it with more blessings/miracles that my family and I have experienced not previously mentioned. Not every single blessing/miracle God has done will be shared because if you think about it, every day that we wake up is a blessing. The ones shared are to give God all the glory and to give you hope because what he does for one person, he will do for another.

The Holy Spirit is part of the trinity: God the Father, God the Son, God the Holy Spirit. In the Old Testament, the term *Holy Spirit* wasn't used much; instead, *Spirit of God* or *Spirit of the Lord* was said. His first mention was right at the beginning.

> *The earth was formless and empty, and darkness covered the deep waters. And the Spirit of God was hovering over the surface of the waters. (Gen. 1:2)*

In the cases of Baleem, Othniel, and Jephtah, the Holy Spirit came upon them for specific tasks but it doesn't give any answer to how long the Spirit stayed on them. However, with Samson, it gives us a hint because three separate times the Spirit came upon him, showing the Spirit didn't stay with him.

> *By now Balaam realized that the Lord was determined to bless Israel, so he did not resort to divination as before. Instead, he turned and looked out toward the wilderness, where he saw the people of Israel camped, tribe by tribe. Then the Spirit of God came upon him, and this is the message he delivered: "This is the message of Balaam son of Beor, the message of the man whose eyes see clearly, the message of one who hears the words of God, who sees a vision from the Almighty, who bows down with eyes wide open. (Num. 24:1–4)*

> *But when the people of Israel cried out to the Lord for help, the Lord raised up a rescuer to save them. His name was Othniel, the son of Caleb's younger brother, Kenaz. The Spirit of the Lord came upon him, and he became Israel's judge. He went to war against King Cushan-rishathaim of Aram, and the Lord gave Othniel victory over him. (Judg. 3:9–10)*

> *At that time the Spirit of the Lord came upon Jephthah, and he went throughout the land of Gilead and Manasseh, including Mizpah in Gilead, and from there he led an army against the Ammonite. (Judg. 11:29)*

> *At that moment, the Spirit of the Lord came powerfully upon him, and he ripped the lion's jaws apart with his bare hands. He did it as easily as if it were a young goat. But he didn't tell his father or mother about it. (Judg. 14:6)*

Then the Spirit of the Lord came powerfully upon him. He went down to the town of Ashkelon, killed thirty men... (Judg. 14:19)

As Samson arrived at Lehi, the Philistines came shouting in triumph. But the Spirit of the Lord came powerfully upon Samson, and he snapped the ropes on his arms as if they were burnt strands of flax, and they fell from his wrists. Then he found the jawbone of a recently killed donkey. He picked it up and killed 1,000 Philistines with it. (Judg. 15:14–15)

In 1 Samuel 10, Samuel anoints Saul as king and tells Saul what he is about to experience and then it is fulfilled in the following verses:

As Saul turned and started to leave, God gave him a new heart, and all Samuel's signs were fulfilled that day. When Saul and his servant arrived at Gibeah, they saw a group of prophets coming toward them. Then the Spirit of God came powerfully upon Saul, and he, too, began to prophesy. (1 Sam. 10:9–10)

From my understanding of scripture and what God has showed me, the Spirit needs a right heart in order to dwell in a person, which is why God had to change Saul's heart. This is also why when Saul got prideful and turned from God, the Spirit departed from him.

Now the Spirit of the Lord had left Saul... (1 Sam. 16:14)

So as David stood there among his brothers, Samuel took the flask of olive oil he had brought and anointed David with the oil. And the Spirit

of the Lord came powerfully upon David from that
day on… (1 Sam. 16:13)

Create in me a clean heart, O God. Renew a
loyal spirit within me. Do not banish me from your
presence, and don't take your Holy Spirit from me.
(Ps. 51:10–11)

David received the Spirit of God to empower him to be king
since Saul was no longer fit. Psalm 51 is said to be after David sinned
with Bathsheba, and he realized he wronged and was asking God's
forgiveness so that he doesn't end up like Saul. Now we have to take
this in context of the old covenant. Before Christ, things worked
differently. They had to make sacrifices constantly for their sins, but
Jesus was the ultimate sacrifice to cover *all* sins. His sacrifice allows
us to have a much different relationship with God.

And I will give you a new heart, and I will put
a new spirit in you. I will take out your stony, stub-
born heart and give you a tender, responsive heart.
And I will put my Spirit in you so that you will
follow my decrees and be careful to obey my regula-
tions. (Ezek. 36:26–27)

And he has identified us as his own by placing
the Holy Spirit in our hearts as the first installment
that guarantees everything he has promised us. (2
Cor. 1:22)

And now you Gentiles have also heard the
truth, the Good News that God saves you. And
when you believed in Christ, he identified you as his
own by giving you the Holy Spirit, whom he prom-
ised long ago. The Spirit is God's guarantee that he
will give us the inheritance he promised and that he

*has purchased us to be his own people. He did this
so we would praise and glorify him. (Eph. 1:13–14)*

I have heard many teachings on how one must ask for the Holy
Spirit to come into their life and be baptized into the Holy Spirit as if
it's something separate that happens from when you are born again.

This simply, according to Scripture, is not the truth. Now the
first believers did have to wait for the Holy Spirit to come upon
them because, first, Christ had to ascend into heaven in order for the
outpouring to happen. They don't have to ask for it; they just follow
Jesus's instructions to wait for the Holy Spirit to come.

*Once when he was eating with them, he com-
manded them, "Do not leave Jerusalem until the
Father sends you the gift he promised, as I told you
before. John baptized with water, but in just a few
days you will be baptized with the Holy Spirit." But
you will receive power when the Holy Spirit comes
upon you. And you will be my witnesses, telling people about me everywhere-in Jerusalem, throughout
Judea, in Samaria, and to the ends of the earth."
(Acts 1:4–5, 8)*

*On the day of Pentecost all the believers were
meeting together in one place. Suddenly, there was
a sound from heaven like the roaring of a mighty
windstorm, and it filled the house where they were
sitting. Then, what looked like flames or tongues
of fire appeared and settled on each of them. And
everyone present was filled with the Holy Spirit
and began speaking in other languages, as the Holy
Spirit gave them this ability. (Acts 2:1–4)*

*Peter replied, "Each of you must repent of your
sins and turn to God, and be baptized in the name
of Jesus Christ for the forgiveness of your sins. Then*

HOLY SPIRIT AND BLESSINGS

you will receive the gift of the Holy Spirit." (Acts 2:38)

Now some may say what about this:

> *When the apostles in Jerusalem heard that the people of Samaria had accepted God's message, they sent Peter and John there. As soon as they arrived, they prayed for these new believers to receive the Holy Spirit. The Holy Spirit had not yet come upon any of them, for they had only been baptized in the name of the Lord Jesus. Then Peter and John laid their hands upon these believers, and they received the Holy Spirit. (Acts 8:14–17)*

To understand this, one has to look at the situation as a whole. This was a unique situation because this is the first of the Gentiles receiving the Holy Spirit. They were told about Jesus by Philip, who was not an apostle. Peter and John were apostles, and this was a significant moment. It was fulfilling what Jesus said in Acts 1:8 about going into Samaria. In order to make sure these Samaritans were counted as part of the church, it was needed that the apostles took part in them receiving the Spirit. It is noted to be the same one all others had received.

Now that it was known Gentiles really could receive the Holy Spirit, Peter understood what was happening during Acts 10.

Even as Peter was saying these things, the Holy Spirit fell upon all who were listening to the message. The Jewish believers who came with Peter were amazed that the gift of the Holy Spirit had been poured out on the Gentiles too.

> *For they heard them speaking in other tongues and praising God. (Acts 10:44–46)*

When one hears the Good News and believes in Jesus Christ, God counts you as his own at that time and gives you the Holy

Spirit. At the moment of being born again, the Holy Spirit comes into you because now there is a place for him to dwell and lead you. This is shown in the scriptures I have already shared: 2 Corinthians 1:22, Ephesians 1:13–14, and in the following:

> *Some of us are Jews, some are Gentiles, some are slaves, and some are free. But we have all been baptized into one body by one Spirit, and we all share the same Spirit. (1 Cor. 12:13)*

> *But you are not controlled by your sinful nature. You are controlled by the Spirit if you have the Spirit of God living in you. (And remember that those who do not have the Spirit of Christ living in them do not belong to him at all.) (Rom. 8:9)*

Receiving the Holy Spirit needs not to be confused with receiving gifts from the Holy Spirit. First to come was the pouring of the Holy Spirit on the people, which allowed for the gifts of the Spirit to come more freely and stay.

> *Then, after doing all those things, I will pour out my Spirit upon all people. Your sons and daughters will prophesy. Your old men will dream dreams, and your young men will see visions. (Joel 2:28)*

> *There is no longer Jew or Gentile, slave or free, male and female. For you are all one in Christ Jesus. (Gal. 3:28)*

Those two scriptures plus 1 Corinthians 12:13 clearly state that the Holy Spirit is for *all* people. Anyone, male or female, that accepts Christ as Lord and Savior will be baptized in the Holy Spirit. The Holy Spirit, being the same spirit in everyone, then has the ability to give any of the gifts of the Spirit to anyone.

*And God confirmed the message by giving
signs and wonders and various miracles and gifts of
the Holy Spirit whenever he chose. (Heb. 2:4)*

*And everyone present was filled with the Holy
Spirit and began speaking in other languages, as the
Holy Spirit gave them this ability. (Acts 2:4)*

Greek word *glóssa* can be translated "tongues" or "languages" as it is in this translation. Nowadays, and even when Paul wrote 1 Corinthians, people speaking in tongues were thought to be people speaking in a language no one could understand. That is not always the case.

*At that time there were devout Jews from every
nation living in Jerusalem. When they heard the
loud noise, everyone came running, and they were
bewildered to hear their own languages being spoken by the believers. (Acts 2:5–6)*

I haven't personally experienced it but have heard several sto-ries/testimonies about someone praying or speaking in tongues in a church and someone else in that church hears them in their native language. When a gift of tongues is used, there might not be an inter-pretation of "The Lord says." It might just be a personal message for someone especially an unbeliever just like what happened in Acts.

More on tongues later. Right now I want to finish showing that the gifts of the Spirit are from God and are only given when and to who he decides to. Hebrews 2:4 and Acts 2:4 already state this. Paul confirms it with the following:

*It is the one and only Spirit who distributes all
these gifts. He alone decides which gift each person
should have. (1 Cor. 12:11)*

While it is the Holy Spirit that makes the ultimate decision, it is fine to ask to receive certain gifts. However, it should be done with the right heart, not out of jealousy or to be the center of attention, but out of the desire to truly help others and spread the good news of Christ.

So you should earnestly desire the most helpful gifts. But now let me show you a way of life that is best of all. (1 Cor. 12:31)

God has given each of you a gift from his great variety of spiritual gifts. Use them well to serve one another. Do you have the gift of speaking? Then speak as though God himself were speaking through you. Do you have the gift of helping others? Do it with all the strength and energy that God supplies. Then everything you do will bring glory to God through Jesus Christ. All glory and power to him forever and ever! Amen. (1 Pet. 4:10–11)

There are different kinds of spiritual gifts, but the same Spirit is the source of them all. There are different kinds of service, but we serve the same Lord. God works in different ways, but it is the same God who does the work in all of us. A spiritual gift is given to each of us so we can help each other. To one person the Spirit gives the ability to give wise advice; to another the same Spirit gives a message of special knowledge. The same Spirit gives great faith to another, and to someone else the one Spirit gives the gift of healing. He gives one person the power to perform miracles, and another the ability to prophesy. He gives someone else the ability to discern whether a message is from the Spirit of God or from another spirit. Still another person is given the ability to speak in unknown languages, while another is

*given the ability to interpret what is being said. (1
Cor. 12:4–10).*

> *All of you together are Christ's body, and each
> of you is a part of it. Here are some of the parts
> God has appointed for the church: first are apostles,
> second are prophets, third are teachers, then those
> who do miracles, those who have the gift of healing,
> those who can help others, those who have the gift of
> leadership, those who speak in unknown languages.
> Are we all apostles? Are we all prophets? Are we all
> teachers? Do we all have the power to do miracles?
> Do we all have the gift of healing? Do we all have
> the ability to speak in unknown languages? Do we
> all have the ability to interpret unknown languages?
> Of course not! (1 Cor. 12:27–30)*

> *Because of the privilege and authority God has
> given me, I give each of you this warning: Don't
> think you are better than you really are. Be honest in
> your evaluation of yourselves, measuring yourselves
> by the faith God has given us. Just as our bodies
> have many parts and each part has a special func-
> tion, so it is with Christ's body. We are many parts
> of one body, and we all belong to each other. In his
> grace, God has given us different gifts for doing cer-
> tain things well. So if God has given you the ability
> to prophesy, speak out with as much faith as God
> has given you. If your gift is serving others, serve
> them well. If you are a teacher, teach well. If your
> gift is to encourage others, be encouraging. If it is
> giving, give generously. If God has given you leader-
> ship ability, take the responsibility seriously. And if
> you have a gift for showing kindness to others, do it
> gladly. (Rom. 12:3–8).*

Well, my brothers and sisters, let's summarize. When you meet together, one will sing, another will teach, another will tell some special revelation God has given, one will speak in tongues, and another will interpret what is said. But everything that is done must strengthen all of you. (1 Cor. 14:26).

Remember that people who prophesy are in control of their spirit and can take turns. For God is not a God of disorder but of peace, as in all the meetings of God's holy people. (1 Cor. 14:32–33)

But be sure that everything is done properly and in order. (1 Cor. 14:40)

To sum up what all these scriptures are saying, first, like other scriptures said, God is the one that gives the gifts. Second, there are many types of gifts, and the ones listed are not all the gifts the Holy Spirit can bestow on someone. There is not one gift that everyone must have or will have. Even similar gifts will present differently because we are designed to be unique and each have their own function to help make the body of Christ work correctly. We are all to work together in growing and building each other up. No one is better than someone else and the same goes for giftings. The different gifts are to work in harmony with each other. The person is in control and should not be disruptive.

I have found over the years that people have a hard time understanding information on the Holy Spirit, partially because, depending on who you talk to, there are a multitude of opinions on it. I do not claim to know everything on it and don't expect you to just take my word on it either. Everyone should read the Bible themselves and ask God to give them revelation on what is being read. This is what I have done. The Holy Spirit revealed to me this information, and I have experienced receiving different gifts of the Spirit. My ability to be able to write this book and share with all is a gift of the Holy Spirit.

Let's talk about speaking in tongues now. There have been numerous times where I heard people tell others that if they don't speak in tongues, they don't have the Holy Spirit and act as if it is a requirement. I have spoken with people that have felt so pressured by others to speak in tongues that they fake it, get discouraged, and are left feeling not good enough. As stated in the scriptures I have already shared and in 1 Corinthians 14 (I recommend reading the whole chapter), this is false information. Not everyone will speak in tongues and being able to doesn't make you more spiritual or better than anyone else. Tongues is a gift from the Holy Spirit that you can open your heart to and ask God for the ability, but it's ultimately up to him.

> *Let love be your highest goal! But you should also desire the special abilities the Spirit gives—especially the ability to prophesy. For if you have the ability to speak in tongues, you will be talking only to God, since people won't be able to understand you. You will be speaking by the power of the Spirit, but it will all be mysterious. But one who prophesies strengthens others, encourages them, and comforts them. A person who speaks in tongues is strengthened personally, but one who speaks a word of prophecy strengthens the entire church. I wish you could all speak in tongues, but even more I wish you could all prophesy. For prophecy is greater than speaking in tongues, unless someone interprets what you are saying so that the whole church will be strengthened. (1 Cor. 14:1–5)*

> *It's the same for you. If you speak to people in words they don't understand, how will they know what you are saying? You might as well be talking into empty space. There are many different languages in the world, and every language has meaning. But if I don't understand a language, I will be a*

foreigner to someone who speaks it, and the one who speaks it will be a foreigner to me. And the same is true for you. Since you are so eager to have the special abilities the Spirit gives, seek those that will strengthen the whole church. So anyone who speaks in tongues should pray also for the ability to interpret what has been said. For if I pray in tongues, my spirit is praying, but I don't understand what I am saying. Well then, what shall I do? I will pray in the spirit, and I will also pray in words I understand. I will sing in the spirit, and I will also sing in words I understand. For if you praise God only in the spirit, how can those who don't understand you praise God along with you? How can they join you in giving thanks when they don't understand what you are saying? You will be giving thanks very well, but it won't strengthen the people who hear you. (1 Cor. 14:9–17)

I remember the day I was blessed with speaking in tongues. I went up during altar call and was so hungry for more of God. Shawn was praying over me, and I felt this fire come over me, and I opened my mouth, and a few noises came out that felt so weird to me. After the experience, I immediately got attacked by the enemy, telling me it was fake, that I just made it up. But I knew I hadn't. For months, when I spoke in tongues while praying, it was just the same thing over and over. Constantly, the thoughts of I was just making it up would torment me and part of me would really question if it was God or if it was me since it was the same thing repeatedly. I had faith that it was God and held on to it. Eventually, new sounds and words came a little bit at a time. There are times to this day I will just repeat the same phrases, and that is okay. I am in control of it. I can start and stop whenever I want. I may not know exactly what I am saying, but that is fine. I have something on my heart I just don't have English words to express, so I speak to God the way I feel is best. I ask for an interpretation of what I am saying in the spirit, and sometimes I just get a feeling or an idea or an image of someone, not necessarily a word-for-word translation. I have been in services wherein someone has spoken in tongues and another person gives the interpretation. I have also been in services wherein things were forced and felt fake and staged. It is important to seek the Holy Spirit for discernment in everything. Do not feel unworthy if you can't speak in tongues or don't get the gifts you see others getting. Don't try to copy what others do either, as if there is a formula that can be followed to receive certain gifts. God made you for a reason, and the reason will be revealed in his timing. Those reasons and ways things are revealed are not always what we would like or expect, but trust that God knows best! We must live a life guided by the Holy Spirit.

So I say, let the Holy Spirit guide your lives. Then you won't be doing what your sinful nature craves. The sinful nature wants to do evil, which is just the opposite of what the Spirit wants. And the Spirit gives us desires that are the opposite of what the sinful nature desires. These two forces are constantly fighting each other, so you are not free to carry out your good intentions. But when you are directed by the Spirit, you are not under obligation to the law of Moses. When you follow the desires of your sinful nature, the results are very clear: sexual immorality, impurity, lustful pleasures, idolatry, sorcery, hostility, quarreling, jealousy, outbursts of anger, selfish ambition, dissension, division, envy, drunkenness, wild parties, and other sins like these. Let me tell you again, as I have before, that anyone living that sort of life will not inherit the Kingdom of God. But the Holy Spirit produces this kind of fruit in our lives: love, joy, peace, patience, kindness, goodness, faithfulness, gentleness, and self-control. There is no law against these things! Those who belong to Christ Jesus have nailed the passions and desires of their sinful nature to his cross and crucified them there. Since we are living by the Spirit, let us follow the Spirit's leading in every part of our lives. Let us not become conceited, or provoke one another, or be jealous of one another. (Gal. 5:16–26)

No matter how many blessings I receive or miracles I see and hear about, I am still in awe of God's goodness with each one. I think a lot of times people like to look at the "big" things/miracles that God does in our lives and don't notice/appreciate as much the "little" things. I think it's the little things that reveal just how much God loves and cares about us. He wants a relationship with us and that we allow him in every part of our life. When we take the time to have that relationship with him, it allows him to guide us with the Holy Spirit through all the little things that truly add up to what matters most and letting his light shine through us to help those that are still lost in the darkness see that there is still hope. There is a light source available that will never turn off. It will be there always to guide you if you just seek and follow it. No matter what you have done, God loves you and wants to be your source. Here are a variety of little and big things God has done for us over the years in no particular order.

*****

During a twenty-one-day corporate fast with my church, I had been praying for my health. About a week into it, Curtis was giving me a back massage when he kept going over an area on my upper back and seemed amazed. I asked him what is going on, and he said, "It's gone." I had a large fibrous mass, kind of like a hump, that he had mentioned before and seemed concerned about. It was no longer there suddenly. He said it was a miracle. There was no way it would have just disappeared on its own. I realized also that I could now put my head further back than I could beforehand. I hadn't even been praying for that specifically, but God healed it.

*****

Four of us were playing Frisbee at the beach, two on the beach and two in the water. I was in the water about waist deep. The waves were a little rough but not too bad. I was on the back side of a shell trough when I got hit with a big rogue wave. It hit my entire back up to my neck and with such force that it slammed me down where my shoulder dug into the ocean floor and proceeded to roll me. When I was able to stand back up, I realized that I couldn't see, which meant my glasses were gone.

I can't function without my glasses and could not afford to replace them. I can read a book in hand, but on my computer screen and everything not within about a foot of my face is blurry, and the further away, the worst it is.

I told my husband and friends that my glasses were gone. They all could have been like, "It's the ocean, you are screwed." I have lost things in the past, and that's how most people seem to react. But my one friend was just like, "Calm down. We all will look." I couldn't even help much not being able to see, but I just immediately starting praying in words and tongues for us to find them, trusting God would do a miracle.

The current was getting pretty rough, after fifteen minutes or so, I heard a scream of joy as one friend found them. He was dragging his feet through the shell trough, lost his balance, and then felt something between his toes. He said it didn't feel like glasses but decided to bring his foot up anyways to see what it was, and it was my glasses!

They were not damaged at all! A little sand was in the nose pieces but no scratches or anything. It was a double miracle, first to find them and then for them to be undamaged. It's the power of prayer and trusting God. He is with you always!

If you feel lost with no hope of being found, God says, "Just like in the natural that it seemed like those glasses were lost with no hope of being found in that huge rough ocean, there is hope!" He sees you, and you are found! There is hope for you in Christ! He won't leave or forsake you!

*****

This testimony may seem silly to some, but to me, it shows how God is in even the smallest things that most would consider insignificant. God really wants to be in every aspect of our lives. So trust him to take care of us.

On our freezer door, it had a water/ice dispenser. The water stopped working a long time ago, and Curtis tried to fix it a few months prior, but it ended up being a much larger project of taking apart the entire freezer door, and he didn't want to do that. One day the kids had apparently played with the buttons on the freezer door, changing it from the ice setting to the water one. I didn't pay attention and just went to get ice when water squirted everywhere. Through this, I felt God saying that, even when things seem against all odds and when you least expect, your miracle/breakthrough will come! Don't lose hope! Trust in God. His plans are the best.

> *Trust in the Lord with all your heart; do not depend on your own understanding. Seek his will in all you do, and he will show you which path to take. (Prov. 3:5–6)*

> *"For I know the plans I have for you," says the Lord. "They are plans for good and not for disaster, to give you a future and a hope. (Jer. 29:11)*

*****

I was having some chest pain and pressure before and during church, so I went up for prayer. The speaker got his wife to come over to me, and she asked if she could pray for me. She seemed nervous, said that she wasn't an eloquent speaker, or good at this. I encouraged her by saying she didn't need special words or lots of practice. She just needed to believe in what she was praying about. If you look throughout scripture, Jesus was simple and to the point in his prayers. It's about knowing what the Holy Spirit can do through you and trusting that! God is my healer, and he can use anyone willing to be the vessel in which he heals through! She prayed for me, and by the time I got back to my seat, I was healed.

> *In one of the villages, Jesus met a man with an advanced case of leprosy. When the man saw Jesus, he bowed with his face to the ground, begging to be healed. "Lord," he said, "if you are willing, you can heal me and make me clean." Jesus reached out and touched him. "I am willing," he said. "Be healed!" And instantly, the leprosy disappeared. (Luke 5:12–13)*

*****

I am thankful I listen to the Holy Spirit and checked my pockets when I did. I was walking into Target with the kids and my phone-wallet combo fell out of my pocket in the parking lot. Thankfully, I found it quickly and unharmed. Remember to listen to his direction!

*****

These last two I will be sharing will both have a series of blessings that all go together and show how God sees the bigger picture and works things for our good.

Curtis was working as an electrician, which he liked doing; however, it was making him travel a lot and be away from home. He had left a prior job because of all the traveling after we had kids because he wanted to be there with us. Another crucial issue with the job was the pay was questionable. One week he got his paycheck deposited, and the next week, it was removed from the account. Thankfully, we hadn't used it yet to pay the bills because that would have been a nightmare. We were looking for something else that was good pay and more local. We put in several applications. He even had a job interview with one and was told he was hired, but it would be a few weeks before he started. About a month later, we see an article online stating that the place he was hired at was actually clos-ing down. While it was upsetting, we trusted God that even though that door was shut, he would open an even better one. In August 2018, Curtis's lifelong friend gave Curtis's resume to the company he worked for, and at the end of the month, Curtis got a call about an interview. His current job at the time made him over fifteen min-utes late for the interview. Not a good first impression. Curtis said despite that, he thought it went well and would be interested in the job. His friend called, got on to him about being late, and told him that he wasn't doing anything special to help him get the job. It was up to the person he interviewed with to make the call. We had faith that if this job was meant to be, then God would work it out. Two weeks later, Curtis got the call that he was hired as an aircraft interior technician. It was exciting. Curtis had wanted to work on airplanes; the job paid well; he would be home nightly; it seemed like it would be in one of the better work environments he had worked out in a while; and, after ninety days, we could get insurance for the whole family. The only issue was the job was thirty to forty-five minutes away from where we were living, and we only had one working vehi-cle. He started the job in October 2018 and loved it. His whole demeanor changed. He seemed happier, less stressed, and he enjoyed going to work.

In March 2019, we got our rent renewal for where we were liv-ing, and they raised the rent to where we couldn't afford to stay. The long drive back and forth to Curtis's work was taking a toll on us too, so we decided it was best to find a place closer to his work. We got a realtor to help us find a place that would work for us. We looked at a dozen different places, but nothing seemed right. Time was closing in to when we had to move, and we wondered if we should just settle for something not as ideal as we had wanted. Then a house came on the market that was cheaper than we were currently paying. It was only seven to ten minutes from his work and had most of the things we had been looking for. We applied for it, got it, and moved in the beginning of May.

As I mentioned in a previous chapter, Curtis suffered from sei-zures in July of 2019. Because of that, he isn't allowed to drive. I would have to take him and pick him up every day with the kids. He worked second shift, which means he wouldn't get off until after midnight. It was such a blessing that we had moved so close to his work just prior to it. I homeschool the kids, and we are on his shift hours, so it isn't a huge deal to have to take him back and forth. He had insurance that helped pay the costs of the medical bills. His job was amazing to him. Also, they have been so understanding and worked with him through all of the issues. It's also the type of job he still can work even with the complications he has had. To this day, I am still beyond grateful for God working everything out to work the way it did.

*****

In the year 2020 when the COVID-19 pandemic started, as I stated in the "Ministry" chapter that the Holy Spirit led me to quit working for the church in January. I had a few prospects of graphic design, website design, and other work, then the pandemic hit, making all of those possible opportunities go away. The stay-at-home order followed by lockdowns made trying to find work nearly impossible. Thankfully, Curtis's job was considered essential. His pay alone was not enough though. Bills were piling up. We didn't have money for food even. Curtis was still having health issues and missing work. I tried not to stress about it, but I had no clue what to do besides pray and trust God to provide like he had in the past so many times.

In the small group I was part of, during one of the Zoom meetings, they asked for prayer requests; and I said for Curtis's health and financial. The group leader prayed, and in his prayer, he asked God specifically for an unexpected check in the mail. Weeks later we receive an envelope with no return info from a different part of the state with a money order for $500 and a piece of paper saying, "For good health." It was signed "The Lord's Army." It was perfect timing, so we could pay bills and get a little food that week.

The pandemic that the enemy meant for evil God worked for good for us. Several of our bill companies worked with us and deferred payments and took away late fees. Unexpected Facebook friends that heard about our struggles and, without even being asked, gave us money to pay the bills that we couldn't defer. Random money blessings happened all year during a year that most were struggling to get by.

My five-year-old son breaks his arm in the middle of the all craziness. I post a photo in the photo group I am part of on Facebook, and someone recommends an herbal supplement that helps with healing. Being honest, I said, "Thanks for the info but right now we can't even afford groceries." That complete stranger that I have never talked to before offers to buy it for us. Another complete stranger saw my comment proceeds to offer to give us some money for groceries!

One week we literally had $4 till the next week, meaning we had no money for groceries or gas. I felt led to clean out a nightstand and found $56. He provides in ways you don't even think about at times! Trust him!

I have tried so many ways to make money to help support my family, trying to sell items on Facebook and on my website. I have tried work-from-home jobs too but with very little success. All I got was stress and disappointment. Due to Curtis's health/work schedule and the kids, I can't get a regular job. I had been praying for God to show me what to do because we kept not having money for groceries or gas, or even to pay some bills. Twice during the same weekend in the end of August, Poshmark was mentioned, and I heard others success stories. It cost nothing but time and effort to try, so I figured why not? After a month of starting, I had nineteen sales from things that I had lying around the house not being used. It hasn't been a lot of money, but every penny is a blessing.

I was seeking the Holy Spirit on what to do since we don't have the money for me to buy clothes secondhand, and I already went through our clothes. I got this in response: how do you know if you don't ask? What harm can there be in asking? Make a post. I did exactly that. I made a post on Facebook and Instagram, being honest and asking people for unused clothes and small household items that I could have to sell. The response I got was overwhelming. My minivan got filled with donations, plus I had some people drive almost two hours to drop off four large garbage bags full of items.

If you help the poor, you are lending to the
Lord—and he will repay you! (Prov. 19:17)

Getting a reward should not be your motivation for giving, but I can testify to you this scripture is truth. Our testimony is that over the years, we have given clothing and other items to those in need because we wanted to help others how we could. We are on the other end now getting blessed. God is faithful and keeps his promises!

We had a cold front come in right after my kids had a growth spurt. Their cold-weather clothes no longer fit them. I made a post not asking for anything just saying that it's insane how in like less than a month how much a kid could grow. Someone I was in Girl Scouts with growing up saw the post and said she wanted to get the kids some clothes. Alone that was just a blessing; however, God didn't stop there. She is a hairstylist and was talking to a client, this client who does not know us gave her a hundred dollars to send to me to buy clothes for my kids. Finally, she had coworkers give her clothes their kids grew out of to mail us.

Sometimes the answers to our prayers take minutes, hours, days, weeks, months, or even years. This particular one only took days. On a Monday, in November, I was seeking God on how we would be able to buy our kids any Christmas gifts this year. By Wednesday night, I got an unexpected answer. Someone we know, mostly through Facebook, sent me a private message asking if it would be okay if she bought our kids some Christmas gifts this year. God laid our family on her heart knowing we have been struggling with my husband's health and all. This moved me to tears. I know her family has had their struggles also, but here she is wanting to bless my family. On top of that, we get an unexpected package from someone we have never met in person. It was full of Christmas presents for the kids. There was even a gift for Curtis and me with a sweet note saying, "We may have never met in person, but your family has brought me joy on social media for years. This year my family wanted to send some holiday love to yours. Thank you for reminding us that no matter what is going on in the world, there is God and faith and love."

I wanted to share this to remind people that no matter how ugly the world is, God loves and cares for you and will use people to remind you of this. Don't give up on God or people. There are plenty of good people out there. It's just they aren't as loud as the others because they do it from the kindness of their heart and not for attention.

We are at the end of the year, and while Curtis's health is not where we would like it to be, it has improved greatly from the beginning of the year. My side business of selling items online including handcrafted ones, which I have always wanted to do, is slowly growing. We have been able to pay our bills, have a roof over our heads, have a working vehicle and food on our table—all thanks to the blessings of God!

I want to remind you today God loves you and knows your needs and will use people you know and don't know to show that love and provide for those needs! If he would do it for us, trust that he will do it for you too! Just seek and ask him!

*****

While this is where this book ends, it is not the end of my journey. The journey will continue till the day I go to be with Jesus in heaven. I pray that everyone that reads this book has gotten something out of it that will help them on their journey. For the readers that haven't started their journey with Christ, I pray that this book has helped you to see God's love for you and for you to make the decision to start your journey by either using the prayer shared in the "Salvation" chapter or just saying it in your own way. God bless you all!

About the Author

Stephanie Anderson has dealt frequently with weather that can be bright and sunshiny one minute, then dark and stormy the next living in Florida. This can be quite similar to how life is.

Stephanie has attended several different types of church over the years. She has helped plant two churches and worked in church administration and creative design for nine years.

Stephanie is a wife and mother of two kids on earth and three in heaven. While *Uniquely Made* is her first book, she has been writing about her faith on blogs for over ten years.

For more information on her and her writings, visit writersa.info.